ANDY JACKSON was born in Salford, England in 1965, but has lived in Scotland since 1993. His two poetry collections *The Assassination Museum* (2010) and *A Beginner's Guide to Cheating* (2015) were both published by Red Squirrel Press, and he has curated and edited several poetry anthologies including *Split Screen* (2012) and *Double Bill* (2014) for Red Squirrel Press, and *Whaleback City: The Poetry of Dundee and its Hinterland* (with W N Herbert) for Dundee University Press (2013). In 2015 he again collaborated with W N Herbert on the *New Boots & Pantisocracies* poetry blog project, chronicling the UK in the months following the 2015 General Election. He was Makar to the Federation of Writers Scotland in 2017.

BRIAN JOHNSTONE was born in Edinburgh in 1950, but has lived in rural Fife since the 1970s. A poet, writer and performer, his work has appeared throughout Scotland, elsewhere in the UK, in North America, Australasia and across Europe. He has published six collections, most recently *Juke Box Jeopardy* (Red Squirrel, 2018) and *Dry Stone Work* (Arc, 2014). His poems have been translated into over a dozen languages. In 2015 his work was selected to appear on the Poetry Archive website. His memoir *Double Exposure* was published by Saraband in 2017. A founder and former Director of StAnza: Scotland's International Poetry Festival, he was a literary events organiser for over 20 years, co-founding Edinburgh's Shore Poets and curating Cave Readings for the Pittenweem Arts Festival in the 1990s. *www.brianjohnstonepoet.co.uk*

Other books by Andy Jackson:

Poetry
*A Beginner's Guide to Cheating*, Red Squirrel Press, 2015
*The Assassination Museum*, Red Squirrel Press, 2010

As Editor
*Seagate III*, Discovery Press, 2016
*New Boots and Pantisocracies*, Smokestack Press, 2016
*Double Bill*, Red Squirrel Press, 2014
*Whaleback City: The poetry of Dundee and its hinterland*, Dundee University Press, 2013
*Tour de Vers*, Red Squirrel Press, 2013
*Split Screen*, Red Squirrel Press, 2012

Other books by Brian Johnstone:

Memoir
*Double Exposure*, Saraband, 2017

Poetry
*Juke Box Jeopardy*, Red Squirrel Press, 2018
*Dry Stone Work*, Arc Publications, 2014
*The Book of Belongings*, Arc Publications, 2009
*Terra Incognita*, L'Officina (Vincenza) 2009
*Homing*, The Lobby Press, 2004
*Robinson: A Journey*, Akros, 2000
*The Lizard Silence*, Scottish Cultural Press, 1996

As Editor
*The Golden Goose Hour*, Taranis Books, 1994

# Scotia Extremis

Poems from the extremes of Scotland's psyche

Edited by
ANDY JACKSON and BRIAN JOHNSTONE

**Luath** Press Limited
EDINBURGH
www.luath.co.uk

This book is dedicated to the memory of *Scotia Extremis* contributors John Mackie and Janet Paisley.

First published 2019

ISBN: 978-1912147-56-4

The authors' right to be identified as author of this book under the Copyright, Designs and Patents Act 1988 has been asserted.

The paper used in this book is recyclable. It is made from low chlorine pulps produced in a low energy, low emission manner from renewable forests.

Printed and bound by
Bell & Bain Ltd, Glasgow

Typeset in 11 point Sabon by Main Point Books, Edinburgh

© the contributors 2019

# Contents

Introduction    11
Scotland: A Split Personality?    12

**WHIGMALEERIES**

*Lydia Robb*
    The Saltire    1
*Sheena Blackhall*
    The Lion Rampant    15
*Jacob Polley*
    A Cultural Landscape    16
*Vicki Feaver*
    Melancholy Thistle, Garvald Quarry    17
*Christine De Luca*
    The White Heather Club    18
*Pippa Little*
    The People's Friend    19
*Mandy Haggith*
    Tweed    20
*Magi Gibson*
    The First Recorded Case    21
*Liz Niven*
    Glasgow Empire    22
*Colin Begg*
    I Remember Your First Time    24
*David Kinloch*
    A Veesion    26
*Claire Askew*
    Nessie to the Unaccompanied Minor    28

**FOWK**

*Richie McCaffery*
    Hamish Henderson (1919–2002)    30
*Colin McGuire*
    Work! Consume! Die!    31
*Dawn Wood*
    Storm in a Teacup, Catterline    32
*Marjorie Lotfi Gill*
    Millennium Window    33

*Catriona Lexy Campbell*
   Farpais A200/ Competition A200     34
*Beth McDonough*
   Prepare to Climb Your Muriel     36
*Stephanie Green*
   Ivor Cutler     37
*Angus Peter Campbell*
   William Topaz McGonagall     39
*W N Herbert*
   Mastercriminal     40
*Tracey Herd*
   Bible Joanne     43
*Rob A Mackenzie*
   To Be John Knox     46
*James Robertson*
   Wee Bozzy Boswell     48

THON PLACE

*Robert Crawford*
   To Sullom Voe     52
*Kate Armstrong*
   Scapa Flow, 2016     53
*Aiko Greig*
   Taking My Mother to Higher Ground     54
*Jacqueline Thompson*
   The In Pin     55
*A C Clarke*
   The Barras     56
*Tessa Berring*
   Caryatid     57
*Nikki Robson*
   The Callanish Stones     58
*Hamish Whyte*
   Little Sparta     59
*James McGonigal*
   Headwaters     62
*Matthew Fitt*
   Spey     63
*Lindsay Macgregor*
   Skara Brae     64
*Marion McCready*
   Polphail Village     65

*Rody Gorman*
  Guth Ri Ràdh/ Nothing to be Said                67
*Gerry Loose*
  Gruinard                                        69

BILL O FARE

*Elspeth McLean*
  Ena Baxter Soup                                 73
*Russell Jones*
  Masala                                          74
*Fran Baillie*
  Uisge Beatha                                    75
*Claudia Daventry*
  Commotion Lotion                                76
*Rebecca Sharp*
  The Declaration of Barrbru                      78
*Dilys Rose*
  Cullen Skink                                    80
*John Glenday*
  The Numbers Stations                            81
*Jean Atkin*
  Edinburgh Castle Rock                           82

GAUN ABOOT

*Stewart Conn*
  The Clockwork Orange                            84
*Donny O'Rourke*
  The Vital Spark                                 85
*Ian McDonough*
  John o'Groats                                   87
*Imtiaz Dharker*
  Mobarik Picnic                                  88
*Janette Ayachi*
  Sauchiehall Street                              90
*Alasdair Paterson*
  The Royal Mile                                  92
*Ian Crockatt*
  The Bridge Over The Atlantic                    93
*Judith Taylor*
  Forth Bridge Calligramme                        94

THE GEMM

*Richard Watt*
   George Kidd    98
*Tom Pow*
   Ken Buchanan (1945–)    100
*Jim Mackintosh*
   Unner the Fold    103
*Maoilios Caimbeul / Myles Campbell*
   Rèisean, Weihsian, Nollaig 1944 / Races, Weihsian, Christmas 1944    104
*Harry Smart*
   4    106
*Graham Fulton*
   Archie Gemmill Scores in a Parallel Universe    108
*Maggie Rabatski*
   When I Hear Your Name, Bill McLaren    110
*Brian Whittingham*
   Arthur Montford's Horizontal Hold    112

HOOLEY

*Harry Giles*
   The Gay Gordons    114
*Andrew J Wilson*
   Vambo Unbound    115
*Andrew Greig*
   Jimmy Shand    116
*Ian Stephen*
   Tales of Brave Ulysses    117
*Janet Paisley*
   Voice    119
*Valerie Thornton*
   Susan Magdalene    120
*Jim C Wilson*
   The Alexander Brothers Perform at the Dean Bowling Club,
   Comely Bank, Edinburgh, June 1971    122
*Theresa Muñoz*
   Men    123
*Kevin Reid*
   Postcard    124
*J L Williams*
   A Rush A Kiss A Rush    125

*George T Watt*
   Niel Gow    126

*Stuart A Paterson*
   Nae Regrets    127

*Eleanor Livingstone*
   Roads Not Taken, Trousers Not Rolled    128

*Rachel McCrum*
   The Jesus and Mary Chain    129

*Màrtainn Mac an t-Saoir / Martin MacIntyre*
   Dùthchas Beò / Living Tradition    130

*Elizabeth Rimmer*
   You Play the Melody    132

TALES

*Patricia Ace*
   Gregory's Girl    134

*Jane McKie*
   Where's the Door Here?    135

*Sheenagh Pugh*
   True Places    136

*Hugh McMillan*
   Summerisle    138

*John Quinn*
   Oor Wullie    139

*Aonghas MacNeacail*
   Black Bob (say no more)    140

*Keren Macpherson*
   The DunBroch Tapestry    142

*Tim Turnbull*
   Prime    143

*Donald S Murray*
   Chic Murray    144

*Jackie Kay*
   A Day Like Today    145

*Christie Williamson*
   Meeting Demand    146

*Jenni Daiches*
   The Body Snatchers    147

NOTIONS

*Douglas Dunn*
   Cadell (and other Colourists) — 150
*Colin Will*
   In a Good Light — 151
*Gerrie Fellows*
   Memoir Concerning the Transmission of Speech — 152
*Ross Wilson*
   Stooky Bill — 154
*Niall Campbell*
   A Twenty Pound Note — 155
*Ruth Aylett*
   Great Powers: John Napier of Merchiston — 156
*Chris Powici*
   Happens — 158
*Jim Carruth*
   One Proof for Lord Kelvin's Second Law of Thermodynamics — 160
*Ryan Van Winkle*
   Grace — 161
*Roseanne Watt*
   Hamefarin / Homecoming — 162
*Ken Cockburn*
   Bob the Roman — 164
*Sheila Templeton*
   James Keir Hardie — 165
*Brian Johnstone*
   North Britain — 166
*Andy Jackson*
   Caledonia — 167

Biographies — 170
Acknowledgements — 183

# Introduction

THE CONCEPT FOR the Scotia Extremis project is based on two books taking a similar approach to cultural icons. *Split Screen* (2012) and *Double Bill* (2014), both published by Red Squirrel Press and edited by Andy Jackson, featured poems in pairs, each pairing being a contrast between two thematic extremes. A 2015 review of *Double Bill* in Scotland's *Gutter* magazine asked when a Scottish variant on the idea would see the light of day. This rhetorical question sparked interest among the two editors, and developed into a year-long online project taking in 142 poets and writers.

This anthology seeks to explore 'the soul of Scotland' through a selection of the specially commissioned poems from its web-based incarnation. The commissioned poets were each given a topic selected by the editors and asked to come up with a new take on their subject's place in the national psyche. Each topic was paired with another to highlight both their common identities and the extremes of the nation's culture they embodied.

Those invited to participate were either poets from Scotland – though not necessarily living there – or poets resident in Scotland – though not necessarily Scottish. We would like to thank all poets involved for the gifts of their creativity and enthusiasm. Sadly, this book did not have space to include all 142 poems from the more expansive online version of the project, but this book is a fine distillation of that online presence.

The topics and their pairings – which here differ in some instances from their original online pairings – were drawn up by the editors Andy Jackson (an Englishman based in Scotland) and Brian Johnstone (a native Scot). While the list of themes reflects the interests and obsessions of the editors, it is by no means intended to be either comprehensive or balanced. It is hoped, however, that it does pick out some of the most telling strands of the nation's DNA.

*Andy Jackson and Brian Johnstone*
*www.scotiaextremis.wordpress.com*
*February 2019*

# Scotland: a Split Personality?

*I'll ha'e nae hauf-way hoose, but aye be whaur / Extremes meet*
— Hugh MacDiarmid

IF A NATION can be said to have a soul then the soul of the Scottish nation is surely one which is permanently strung out between the extremes that MacDiarmid evokes in what must be one of his most quotable lines. Taken from his great early poem *A Drunk Man Looks at the Thistle*, it seems to sum up both the irascible poet and his nation so well.

It was not, of course, his only foray into examining the split psyche of the country. He also explored the notion of the Caledonian Antisyzygy, a term coined by G Gregory Smith in 1919 to encapsulate the conflicting extremes within the culture of Scotland and which MacDiarmid expanded on in a 1931 essay. In his original essay Smith wrote of Scottish literature as being 'remarkably varied, and becoming, under the stress of foreign influence, almost a zigzag of contradictions.'

Perhaps the most famous examples of this 'split personality' in our country's culture are Robert Louis Stevenson's *Strange Case of Dr Jekyll and Mr Hyde* and James Hogg's *The Private Memoirs and Confessions of a Justified Sinner*. Such dichotomies persist throughout Scottish literary history, however. The rural/urban split goes as far back as the 1480s and Robert Henrysoun's *The Taill of the Uponlandis Mous and the Burges Mous*.

In Scotland, rivalries seem to be almost a given. It is not difficult to think of examples: Edinburgh / Glasgow, Rangers / Celtic, Native Tongue / English, Protestant/Catholic, not to mention Scottish/British that seemed to be the choice presented to Scots in 2014's independence referendum. Within Calvinism, Scotland's very own rigorous form of Protestantism, there is the conflict between the saved – those predestined for heaven – and the eternally damned. Just read Burns's *Holy Willie's Prayer* for elucidation.

The whole split personality of the country is perhaps best seen in two contrasting attitudes with which Scottishness is associated: the posturing of 'wha's like us? – damn few an they're aa deid' and the cultural self-abnegation exemplified by the so-called 'Scottish cringe'. Where else can anyone live – and write – who lives in Scotland other than 'whaur extremes meet'?

*Brian Johnstone, February 2019*

# Whigmaleeries

THE SALTIRE ~ THE LION RAMPANT

HEATHER ~ THISTLE

THE WHITE HEATHER CLUB ~ THE PEOPLE'S FRIEND

TWEED ~ TARTAN

GLASGOW EMPIRE ~ GLASGOW BARROWLAND BALLROOM

HAGGIS ~ NESSIE

THE SALTIRE ~ THE LION RAMPANT

*Few flags could be as contrasting as the national and the royal flags of Scotland. While the Lion Rampant is officially restricted to use by officers of state, the Saltire is flown in numerous public places and sported by revellers worldwide.*

## The Saltire

Stour has settled in the camphor grooves
of my grandmother's old kist.
I prise the sprung padlock from its moorings,

reveal many years of hoarding,
indulge in what my mother called a reenge,
unearthing objects long forgotten.

The conch shell with the sea trapped in its ears,
a rain-stick purchased after too much wine,
sepia snaps of relatives, all gone.

And in an unfamiliar cardboard box,
I find what I've been searching for;
a startling blue and white St Andrews cross,

the scent of jute and resin in its folds.
I feel the warp and weft of it in my hands
and as the dark creeps in to fill your empty shoes,

I'm minded of the promise I made you.
The day will dawn, the flag unfurled. I pause,
reflect on the alchemy of memory and love.

*Lydia Robb*

# The Lion Rampant

We Scots are a free reenge breed
See the diaspora? Like thrissle seeds in a gale
We're aawye, ony wee crack or neuk'll dae
Fur us tae sattle, trailin oor reets
Like navel towes, tied tae Mither Caledonia

Stirling, Bannockburn, Falkirk,
Otterburn, Flodden, Culloden
The bluid o a warrior tribe rins ben oor veins
Bratach rìoghail na h-Alba's
The sail that steers oor boatie.

Hector MacKay in Quebec weirs
The Lion rampant on his t-shirt,
Proodly on Hogmanay

Elroy Zanzibar-Farquharson in Jamaicay
Has stukken a lion magnet on his fridge
*Och ay the noo* he says
As he cracks open anither tinnie

Felicity Menzies jogs aroon New York
Wi a lion rampant frontin the peak o her cap
She ains twa CDs o the Glesga polis pipe band

In Majorca, Rab C. Buchan
Dichts the san frae his taes
Wi a Lion rampant tool

Thon lion gaes aawye
Pencils, shortbreid tinnies, car stickers
It's aa tae dae wi attitude
Nemo me impune lacessit
Mess wi me an I'll batter ye.

*Sheena Blackhall*

*Think of a plant that represents Scotland and 'the noble thistle' onopordum acanthium will inevitably spring immediately to mind. But close behind it must come* calluna vulgaris, *'the bonnie purple heather', whose white form is reputed to bring luck to all who find it.*

## A Cultural Landscape

o bilberry-rich birch wood
o heath understorey

by girsit, by scythin, by fire
thon place is kent

*where pine trees stood*

*Jacob Polley*

# Melancholy Thistle, Garvald Quarry

Your tribe is famous
for its gregariousness
and ferocity.

You're the odd one out –
spikeless, solitary,
a great big softie.

An apothecary's cure
for melancholy,
not melancholy yourself,

a watcher, not a joiner-in,
you stand sentinel
at the edges of fields

shaking your huge
and heavy head
and quietly laughing.

*Vicki Feaver*

*The Melancholy Thistle is said by some to have been the original badge of the House of Stuart, instead of the Cotton Thistle. Garvald Quarry is a stone's throw from Brownsbank where Hugh MacDiarmid wrote* A Drunk Man Looks at the Thistle.

*An early attempt to present Scotland's culture on television,* The White Heather Club *was more akin to a London Caledonian Ball than a traditional ceilidh. Stereotyping from a different angle,* The People's Friend *is the literary equivalent of plain fare.*

## The White Heather Club

For a growing lass veering between *Girl* comic
and *Woman's Weekly*, there was something
about that predictable *Hello! And welcome to
The White Heather Club!* that set more than
feet tapping. This was better than dancing
with your sister. The YouTube version is grainy,
unsteady, and I'm cringing to think that we loved
our dose of that prancey-wancy, shankly-ankly
back, forward and bow, a dressage of dance;
the pretence at casual pairing off in sets,
the coiffured smiles. Who knows, they may
have been stabbing each other in the back
at the end of the show, creating havoc
in their hotel. And the music never let up
that insistent tiddily-diddily. But we tapped along,
were swept up by the men all brilliantined,
swirly kilted, as they Mucked out Geordie's Byre,
not a speck of sharn on their wee pumps,
all pointy *pas de bas*-ing with only a douce hooch!
And we checked out the women too, admired
their flouncy dresses, wondered how they starched
their petticoats and how their back-combed hair
was motionless. It all seemed so wholesome,
so relentlessly cheery, so sexless and so *Schottische*.

*Christine De Luca*

# The People's Friend

*On wings of song* and sweetened with *a breath of country air*
*the story so far* wraps up a cosy scene of happy endings:
The Good Lord won't send us more than we can bear
if we live our lives as *hidden gems*, make do with mending –
*who can resist the soft warmth of flannelette?* Comfort is all
we deserve, desire now, our *piano favourites, simple knits*, a day
                                              made bright;
*problems below the waist*, ageing, loneliness, a fall
soothed with *Reflections from the Manse*, a mail-order baby doll –
                                            what might
hold back the dwindling life, the darkening horizon
if not *clip-on magnifiers*, tasty meal ideas, *Historical Romance*?
Why not? Wasn't Scotland always this way once, *All Our*
                                              *Yesterdays* arising
from *very special moments*, collective Love Darg toil? Only chance
and change conspire to make it wishful longing now from *people*
                                                    *who*
*don't always get the credit they deserve* and keep secrets, too.

    *Pippa Little*

*All phrases in italics are taken from* The People's Friend, *30 January 2016*

TWEED ~ TARTAN

*While tartan is generally regarded as pan-Scottish, its origins lie entirely in the Gaelic culture of the Highlands and Islands. Equally identified with the country (in both senses of the term), tweed acquired its name – although erroneously – from the border river.*

# Tweed

Its rough, red-flecked, silk-lined softness
hangs only in memory. I cannot try it on.

She offered it to me once. My sister too.
Ever tidy, she must have put it to a sale.

So now, although I hunger to shrug it over my shoulders,
put my hands into her pockets, maybe find a 20p,

a tissue to touch or a hankie to hold onto,
there's only a wardrobe to empty

and then a train to catch
back north over the border river

to where that soft-rough fabric came from,
where the big round buttons belong.

*Mandy Haggith*

# The First Recorded Case

The owner of the Highland Guesthouse
on the Banks of the Bonny Braes
– not a Scot by birth –
first dipped his toe, so claims his spouse,
as a marketing device, intended to entice
the tourists in. After all, he said, it works
for oatcakes, rugs and haggises,
for Edinburgh Rock and haberdasheries.

He started with the curtains, a tasteful ancient
Robertson. American guests were wowed.
Soon he'd papered every room, each in a different clan –
modern, hunting, dress. Oh how he beamed
when guests from far Japan bowed down, impressed.

His wife hoped it would stop right there.
But no! What better, he declared, than tartan
carpet underfoot on every floor and stair?
And when soft furnishings failed to satisfy –
he turned to clothes and underwear.

He couldn't see himself in what he called
a man-skirt, but tartan trews to match the dining room
would do the trick. Seamlessly he slid from
harmless predilection to full hardcore addiction.

And then, one night, his wife, off-season, knitting
in the lounge, disquieted by a muffled sound,
looked round and saw, hovering disembodied,
(against the Clan Macgregor Ancient Dress)
her husband's pale moon face, his startled hair
as he became half-man, half-tartan chair.

*Magi Gibson*

*A brace of Glasgow theatres of different eras and reputations. The Empire on Sauchiehall Street was a notoriously difficult house for music hall and variety acts to win over, while the Barrowlands is a rough but prestigious rock venue east of the city centre.*

## Glasgow Empire

*If they liked ye they let ye live.*
A luxury no afforded thae globe-trottin
empire buildin sodgers.

Back hame fear-fillt shoes tread
the theatre's widden boards.
Shoutin fae sherp-tongued audiences.

*See ye at the Depot oan Monday morn,*
*ya wee fat bastard.*
Tae the comic wi a bus drivin day joab.

*Christ, there's two o them,*
Bernie Winter's fissog peerin
throu the curtains efter Mike.

*Bugger aff*, tae the Irishmen
who reversed aff stage singin,
*Right ye are bejabbers.*

*Goodnight all,*
on Des O Connor's soles.
Carried aff efter a feigned faint.

Ice cream flung at a topless act.
A coin lobbed aff Bobby the Maestro's heid.
Ten bob a week extra in danger money.

Victor Seaforth in a cold sweat kennin
he'd tae finish his Charles Laughton Quasimodo.
*Away hame ya humpy-backed aul bastard.*

Till nae turn was unstaned an the tide turnt.
Duncan Macrae an Albert Finney
strikin demolition's first blows.

Thon tap-tappin echoed ower the globe,
no jist in this country, a wey o life chyngin
boays in tartan bunnets marchin hame.

Colonels packin in thir ain wee Empires,
fortunes made in far flung places.
Noo mair nor an Empire Theatre brekkin tae bits.

*Liz Niven*

# I Remember Your First Time

I took you there sight unseen
last winter touring season –
my South Belfast girl, mixed marriage.
Your blue eyes had never darkened the Gallowgate.

Out past the Sarrie Heid
hugging the north side of the road
your pupils narrowed
at lights blazing: *Barrowland!!*

Past the louts, through the touts,
frisked by stout bouncers,
through the metal detector
up the mirrored stair to the bar:

cheap lager, tacky lino,
ghostly Sixties gauds
and the stale Brut
of Bible John.

\*

After a final sound check,
(one, two    two    p-pow!)
(because roadies can't count to three...)
the bands always start
       with a darkness
       a stage of shadows
       a spreading cheer
       a press-forwards
       lights! anticipation! feedback!
We find a place, on the left.

*The Jesus and Mary Chain play
Psychocandy Live* is fuzz fuzz, whirling wires,
white persistence,
smoke, smoke and twisting ire,
melted-down vocals.

Time dilates and spreads –
through jumpsweat of crowd,
starry ceiling, bouncy floor, faint piss,
nose-tang of smoke machine smoke,
comes olfactory roll call of
        lovers lost
        bands seen
        friends missed
        old stubs in my scrapbook.
        sweet spill of beer.

You turned with a barbed wire kiss,
caught my mood:
moving up and still alive,
still like honey.

    *Colin Begg*

## HAGGIS ~ NESSIE

*Rarely sighted in the wild, the Haggis is unique in having two legs shorter than the others from continually running round the sides of mountains. Not until the invention of the camera did Nessie show up much. Maybe the creature was waiting for its close-up.*

## A Veesion

*Bein a post-Brexit owresettin o the poem Une Charogne by Charles Baudelaire. Wi bits missed oot.*

D'ye mind yon thingummy we seen, hen,
wan mochie back-end day:
jist at the kink o the close, a collop o flesh
jirbled its guts wi a blasé
an cynical wink: a haggis
impaled oan the rail.

It dreeplt an drappit
an grat an slittered,
turned the stairfit intae a stew,
an aw the midgies and maukies
that steyed up the close
thocht heiven had come tae the Drum.

They crowled oan the tripe.
They fucked in the thairms.
They mooched in the painch.
The skin roiled oan its ane.
An the stink! The stink
was a stink lik a stank.

Och wha cud blame the wee dug
– Mrs Henderson's pug –
fur startin a tug-o-war.
You tugged an it tugged,
we aw tugged thegither
an the haggis jauped fae its poke.

Ma angel, ma passion, hale countries
o offal tottered ooty the close
an ah hud a veesion o transmugrification:
ma luv a huge haip o a haggis,
– yon bonnie lichts an heid cheese –
in aw the lingos o Europe.

There are yer tootsies ah sae luv tae suck:
Latin pajata an Romany drob;
yer tummy is trippa, yer airms herzgulasch,
yon bubbies are – aw man – jist lampredotto,
yer throat's a rerr rognon
an yer neb's andouillette.

Lass, len me yer blood tongue,
auld Scoatland's haggis creole,
Atlantic papiamento.
In time o need your meats
are whaur extremes meet
a fleur o Europe at the close stairheid.

*David Kinloch*

# Nessie to the Unaccompanied Minor

Like you, I was unmoored – all my kind
dying – and like you, I'd heard
there may be safe port in this land.
The bottle of the sea loch stoppered.
I watched its neck – through millennia
quick as an eyeblink – narrow, narrow
and I could not move. I was not like you:
couldn't trust my heart, my own
little outboard motor.

But like you, I know what it means
to be hunted: to have nets cast
in your wake, nets barbed
with all the ways they'd like to take
you apart. Out, they send their boats
to find us: out, and out. The search-
lights glitter on the loch like spilt fuel.
As if we don't know boltholes! The art
of disappearing oneself among the rocks.

(They want to find us, but
they also do not.)

Monster to tabloid monster: I'm sorry –
you're starting a loneliness I know
only too much of. This loch
is a big drum I rattle through,
fin over fin, flick over seized old tail sick
of swimming. I'm singing, if
you can bear to be near water
any more. The song goes
*alone, alone, alone –*

but you know that.
It's the only song you've ever sung.

*Claire Askew*

# Fowk

HAMISH HENDERSON ~ FRANKIE BOYLE

JOAN EARDLEY ~ EDUARDO PAOLOZZI

ALI ABBASI ~ MURIEL GREY

IVOR CUTLER ~ WILLIAM McGONAGALL

SAWNEY BEAN ~ BIBLE JOHN

JOHN KNOX ~ JAMES BOSWELL

HAMISH HENDERSON ~ FRANKIE BOYLE

*Few contributed more to traditional culture in Scotland than Hamish Henderson. In a nation with a vivid imagination his grounded vision is vital. One of Scotland's most popular stand-ups, Frankie Boyle's controversial style is calculated to shock the audience, but always seeks to confront comfortable received notions.*

## Hamish Henderson (1919–2002)

For me always the Embra of Hamish Henderson
where the dark old side of toun holds some
of the brightest minds full of new ideas
or else the old ideals recast and reset
like Heine's freedom becoming people
becoming, for Henderson, poetry and song,
and all this under the shadow of the Bomb.
He went from the lyrical ego of the war poet

to the anonymous sower of the folk-leid,
yet in every book in his library he scrawled
his name as if to prove that for a while
he bided in a howff of song, ideas and words
imbibing all along but never made insensible.
He took pride not in himself but others –

the fate of the recorder of oral culture
that he recorded so little of himself.

*Richie McCaffery*

# Work! Consume! Die!

To be frank, I am a prick
your mother rode to stave off
the death of your Father's libido.

Rattling the herd morality live,
wielding taboos open blade, plunging
into flat screen realities;

applying an abrasive to the quietness
of family life, to the stable veneer
of a smooth finish.

Scottish folk are so mangled
after a lifetime dedicated to substance
abuse, casual violence and sectarianism

they choose to commit suicide
to save themselves
waiting for death.

I'm pulling a truth stare, point blank
in your direction, toying
with all you've never had the gall to say.

These jokes need a paramedic
to apply the Glasgow Coma Scale
to consciousness after the punchline.

My message is trigger, trigger, trigger;
subtle as a sledgehammer through a megaphone,
to mock a broken world with blunt force trauma.

*Colin McGuire*

## JOAN EARDLEY ~ EDUARDO PAOLOZZI

*Joan Eardley is best known for her portraits of children in the Glasgow slums, but is also acclaimed for the landscapes she painted in Catterline. Eduardo Paolozzi worked in mosaic and glass but it's his imposing statues which stay in the mind's eye.*

## Storm in a Teacup, Catterline

I lost the horizon
my face was smudged with ochre, violet,
charcoal on the heel of my hand

poverty pushed very far –
a sudden sun
how the dust motes celebrate –

if you look – particles of fabric,
one crinkled hair, twirling, like a smile –
dancing in a snow-globe.

What is there to do, but light
the things that crave attention –
chalk dust, a hole in a beehive,

the daisy-eyes of little Pat,
her sisters and the boys,
round faces that blossom;

I push my pram of paint
into the street that noticing creates
a hopscotch path of now –

feet planted – now and now!
the stir of sun –
I swoop with the heel of my hand

once for the cloud
once for the field
storm in a teacup, Catterline

*Dawn Wood*

# Millennium Window

*I have been paying particular attention to the idea of reflecting deep religious experiences objectified or even immortalised in shapes and colour.*
 *– Sir Eduardo Paolozzi, 23 March 1999, on his Millennium Window in St Mary's Cathedral, Edinburgh*


If colour is language
    place the autumn requiem of leaves
beside their honeydewed rebirth,
    the speckled ink of midnight
alongside the pitted skin of winter daylight,
    the clear brine drawn back to sea
next to its return in milky foam;
    whatever the hue, the eye
will see the arc in between.

And for man, the body fallen apart
    and reassembled back into a form
of itself, the five digits of hands
    or feet, the same and different;
after the first break of childhood each
    works to make up the whole
of their cobbled parts, hide
    the cinemagraph between the purity
of our landing, and what is left.

Kneel to pray: the lines cutting across
    palms aligned, mirror images,
equal and not equal, and with closed eyes
    read the garnet map of the body's
inner workings, as the geometry of colour,
    both message and memoir,
flickers on the slabs below.


    *Marjorie Lotfi Gill*

Ali Abbasi came to Scotland in 1963, joining the BBC in the 1980s where he was a strong supporter of Gaelic. He died at the age of 42 in 2004. Muriel Gray, a dedicated hill walker, is a more acerbic commentator, mainly on arts and culture in Scotland and beyond.

# Farpais A200

*Mar chuimhneachan air Ali Abbasi*

Solas òir na grèine
na laigh air copan airgid
is d' ainm air lainnir.

Bàrdachd ga h-aithris,
briathran beò ann an labhairt,
guthan air an tabhachd
do chànan neo-chaillte,
còmhradh a' maireann
le ioma blas-cainnte.

Chan eil farpais eadarainn.

Tha sinn uile a' sìneadh
chun na duais thar phrìs:
caraid a dh' innseas do 'n t-sluaigh
g' eil luach nad fhacail.

*Catriona Lexy Campbell*

# Competition A200

*In memory of Ali Abbasi*

Golden sunlight
resting on a silver cup
and your name sparkling.

Poetry recited,
words living in expression,
voices offered
to an unlost language,
discourse enduring
with many accents.

There is no competition between us.

We are all reaching
for the priceless prize:
a friend who will tell the crowd
that your words have value.

*Catriona Lexy Campbell*

*The Ali Abbasi Memorial Cup is a trophy presented by the Royal National Mòd to Gaelic learners reciting poetry in respect of Abassi's legacy of support for the language.*

# Prepare to Climb Your Muriel

You'd not tabled her
Munro-glam, but check
that summit snow shock. Don't
scale her down, don't reckon on
some shilpit kind of Corbett. Expect

right feisty crags, belays to take
poke elbow turns. There is
no tourist path; she's more
attitude than altitude. Screw
your courage and your

soup flask lid. Shove
your moleskins, shave your beard –
don't think you'll sneak
that back way up a rabbit track
through easygoing glens. A Rowan

springs one woman there, whittle fine
punkbright from East Kilbride (and you should know
she's partly Yiddish). But
tarmac's every chip as tough.
Carved sandstone gives no hold

even to prehensile toes.
Every crevice cracks
opens down her fissure face
as bastard flames scour out
our Toshy's spooked wood dreams.

Mica glistens fierce in granite
to sharp and wit her supple strength. So
chank your belt, now catch that axe,
sling your hooks, clip crampons on –
watch up. Watch out.

No pin, however sharp
is truly inaccessible. For this
more gallus one, pack kit. Allow
some careful recce time. Show
serious respect.

*Beth McDonough*

IVOR CUTLER ~ WILLIAM MCGONAGALL

*Eccentricity is the link; skill is the contrast. Poet/songwriter Ivor Cutler has changed perceptions with his surreal* Life in a Scotch Sitting Room. *William Topaz McGonagall is famed for his clunky lauding of* The Beautiful Railway Bridge of the Silv'ry Tay!.

## Ivor Cutler

A wee figure spot-lit on a dark stage
intoning like a Jewish cantor on your wheezing harmonium,
wearing Tartan, and a sunflower stuck in your beret.

What if the world was remade in your vision?
Shops are lifted, doctors collect their thoughts
from their surgeries.

A Scottish childhood is no longer *gruts* for tea.
No one is beaten by the tawse. A screwed-up
childhood may be good for creativity,

but *borders, easily bored*, we play, just passing
the time, letting our words come out, like jazz,
however they want. Surrealism meets Music Hall.

We all speak quietly. Singers and comedians
are almost inaudible. Chuffed if pauses
are longer than Sam Beckett's.

We meet applause with fingers in our ears.
The wax model of an ear pinned to our walls,
we are all members of the Noise Abatement Society.
Everyone is addressed by their surname
with courtesy, gentleness. *Cups of tea,
you and me* – a beautiful cosmos.

*Stephanie Green*

# William Topaz McGonagall

It was on the Twentieth of November Two Thousand and Fifteen
That I was asked to write a poem about a poet who's been
Grossly calumnied on the Scottish literary scene
Despite his masterpiece about the disaster on the Tay
Which would never have happened if the central girders had not given way
On that fateful day when the lives of all the passengers were taken away.

William Topaz McGonagall was his name
And I hardly need say anything about his world-wide fame
For he was known everywhere, not just in Dundee, but also very far away
In the Fair City of Perth and far out west in lovely Stornoway
Where the people speak in such a strange way,
Probably because they don't live near the beautiful silv'ry Tay.

Now you may sit there and scoff but it takes balls of steel
To rhyme like McGonagall as he sat on Law Hill
Looking down on Lochee sitting bonny and still
And to the north, Broughty Ferry and then Kirriemuir
Where the peewits were singing so bright and so pure
That a man who was deaf would be made well and cured.

Now of Scotland's great writers I'll just mention a few:
Dunbar, for example, but most of all Hugh
MacDiarmid, who changed his name from Christopher Murray Grieve
And lived for a while in Montrose, which is just north of Dundee, I believe.
And also Burns who liked to rhyme
Though he died very young and therefore didn't get much time.

William Topaz McGonagall, I salute your crazy courage.
The hopeless belief that rhyme was all that mattered
That words could be squeezed into shape, battered
Into submission. All praise to your insane scansion and metres,
The mad joy of your verse, with its strange discordant beat:
Great poetry is always made by holy fools whaur extremes meet.

*Angus Peter Campbell*

SAWNEY BEAN ~ BIBLE JOHN

*Infamous murderers both, Sawney Bean being the 16th century head of a cannibalistic Ayrshire clan, and Bible John the Glasgow serial killer from the late 1960s, presumed to have escaped justice and whose real identity has never been proved.*

## Mastercriminal

The Denfiends and thi clan o Bean
baith hud ae ugsome mission:
tae eat aa Scotia, fat or lean,
in a cook-aff competition.

Thi Denfiends bideit beh Monikie,
thi Beans beh Ballantrae:
wan liked tae sup oan fowk-a-leekie,
wan munched man fricassee.

Thir contest wiz baith comprehensive
and, cuisine-wise, a stretch –
thi ingredients, tho inexpensive,
cuid be a pain tae fetch.

Thi thrie estates, fae nyaff tae laird,
wi ilka ane ae dish,
thrie different weys maun be prepared
(thi clergy coonts as fish.)

Thi Beans began wi Broth MacBeth
a sort of cullage skink
but steeped in bluid and biled tae death –
thi newt ehz clogged thir sink.

Thi Denfiends trehd John Knoxtail soup
but thi keest wiz unca werish:
dreh Calvin croutons, brimstane gloop –
yir parish, parched, wid perish.

The Beans cooked Connery confit
in a nesht o shumwan'sh hair,
anna terrine wha's sheen wiz medd complete
beh thi een o Logie Baird.

The Denfiends favoured finger food –
we presume Dyte Livingstone's;
thir Slessor sliders luked dead good;
Brude's bridies, overdone.

Ane barbecued Rabbie wi Fergusson fritters
inna greasy bardic freh;
thi tither geed ye literary skitters
wi Sir Walter Scottage peh.

Ane served a Parcel o Rogues ragout
wi a dhansak o Dundas;
thi tither's chilli con Darnley blew
thi madrigals oot yir arse.

Thi ashets struck thi board as fast
as Crocketts cuid be spatched,
as Grassic Gibbon's giblets hashed,
or Naomi's limbs detached:

Chic Murray Kiev inna bunnet because
his entrance shidna be cauld;
braised Nesbitt brains in Rab C sauce
laid oan a heidband's fauld;

Scotch eggs de Mary Queen o Scots,
in a lochan o hur gravy;
fresh Para Handy hough in pots;
a Hume-elette o Davie;

wee Lulu in a goulash – aw!
Mock Chop MaGreegor – service!
Sir Alex haggised in a baw –
but noo baith teams luked nervous...

Thi Denfiends hud few pastry skills,
and Sawney feart desserts –
besides, they werr rinnin short on kills,
while Scotland grew alert...

Thir John Broon broonies'd scunner Vic,
lyk thir sponge wi Gilfillan fillin;
while thir Reverend Thomas Spottit Dick
wad find few puntirs willin.

While thi hooves o thi militia scuffed
thir wey tae Desperate Den,
King Duncan doughnuts n Plum McDuff
wiz scoffed beh cannibal men.

And while, thir flintlocks cocked, they moshed
at thi entrance tae thon antre,
a battered Macintosh wiz noshed
wi anthropophagic banter.

Thi order geean, whit they were seean
wad stow a stervin soo,
fur boady pairts, in ilka airt,
werr prinklin inna stew;

werr prinklin, sizzlin, steamin – cooked,
or in man-marinades:
thi wabbit sodgers luked n puked
and fired aff enfilades.

They shucked thi Beans wi baignets fixed,
wi cordite choked thi cave;
thi Denfiends wi thir dennir mixed,
an but wan bairn wiz saved.

O hur latter life ye micht huv heard:
she entered politics,
whaur, haund tae myth, they eat oor words
till truth itsel is sick.

But whit thi people, unappalled,
wad ken, fur Scotland's sake,
is wha's oor Maister Cannibal –
results, eftir this break...

*W N Herbert*

# Bible Joanne

I     Joanne

Her parents were strict. She left school at 14.
She gave them half her wages. Her clothes
were cheap: bargain nylons, dowdy headscarves.
She was only allowed out at weekends
and had to be home by midnight. Her mother insisted.
She met a strange, wee man she could construct
a stage and theatre from, for all the drama
she intended. An occasional prompt but otherwise silence.
*You'll be wanting children soon. You'll be wanting children soon.*
She hated his mother and four sisters as she hated her own.
Her anger grew as the baby grew inside her. Instinctively,
she knew it was a girl and it was draining her blood.
She could still smell a menstruating woman, sick as she felt.
*Thou shalt cast them away as a menstruous cloth* (Isaiah 30:22)
Such a plan! Should it be The Majestic or The Barrowlands?
No matter. Their handbags all held the accoutrements
of a whore – stringent perfume, red, blue, black pigments, coins.


II     Feb 1996–Sept 2010

Strange to think that Glasgow is the Gaelic word for *green hollow.*
Now it was packed with sturdy building blocks of industry, universities,
looming but beautiful buildings, *dens of iniquity…*
On a brilliant, raw morning thirty or so years later, an exhumation.
*Across from the watchers… a polythene tent, crusted in ice*
*stands at the edge of the graveyard at the top of the hill*
*above Stonehouse, and from it the sounds howl…*
*a pneumatic drill gouging at the frozen earth…* this bloodless gash.
The bones are of little use however and the poor corpse may be blameless.
The original DNA found on the girl is too degraded, as blurry
as the ghostly picture of a neo-natal scan, breath rasping in the bitter air.
Once again, he has 'disappeared'. A woman, in her fifties,
thin-lipped, eyes alert, stands at a distance, quite invisible.

In September 2010, the last living witness, her claim to unwanted fame,
to the man known as 'Bible John', 'lucky' Jean McLachlan
who shared a taxi halfway home with her sister Helen Puttock
left this world of sinners. She had been brought in at least
250 times to view suspects. She hadn't spoken to her ex
brother-in-law since 1969. It was a relief to die and leave
the dance-hall of horrors, the drunken, exuberant, red, gold,
orange lights, star shapes and faces shooting off into the night.
In daylight, they were grim, twisted wire hieroglyphs of steel,
leeched of colour. Workers walked past the grubby edifice,
a woman without her bright garments, make-up and curls.
*Lights so bright must, by definition, cast shadows.*
Oh Jeanie, which is Hell and which is Heaven?


III    22nd Feb 1968–31st October 1969

It was a pleasant conversation. Her name was Patricia,
her husband was in the army, down South. She admired her
orange, crocheted dress. Facially, they were mirror images.
She was a nursing auxiliary. Her period cramps were 'terrible'.
She was found two days later in a lane near her home
by a cabinet maker, a creator who stumbled on destruction.
She was naked, raped, and strangled with her own nylons.
*He has made naked her fountain and she has uncovered
the fountain of her blood.* (Leviticus 20:18)
Her handbag, emptied out, was discarded, its open mouth
that soil and weeds and stones would cram full if left.

Three children and unmarried. She bit down hard enough
on her lip to draw blood. Slut. She had one child now, a girl.
She barely caught her name: 'I'm Jemima McDonald'.
She was 5ft 7" with dyed brown hair. She disgusted her.
She'd left home with her curlers in her hair under a red scarf
and come straight to the toilets to make herself a whore.
Her scarf lay pooled on the grubby space by the sink.
Soon enough she would be stretched out on metal
being cleansed of all sin before being cut open.
She had just begun to menstruate. Joanne had towels
in her bag. 'Oh thank you. You're a lifesaver. I didn't

expect it so soon.' She watched her carefully and coveted
with all her being the black pinafore dress, white ruffled
blouse, the off-white sling back shoes. This time, however
he messed up, leaving her fully clothed. He was too frenzied,
raping her then strangling her with her own nylons. Again. Again.
She sulked for weeks about the pinafore dress. He swore
he'd make it up to her. She thought of the grubby children
exploring the empty tenement telling wild stories about a body.

Helen Puttock always made her giggle. The false identikit,
her sister's drunken remembrance of the taxi ride.
A tall man! Red-haired. He was so small and mousey. She knew
he was soft spoken though as he'd repeated the nonsense
she'd scripted for him. Let her suffer, forever guilty,
leaving her sister alone with a strange man.
*We are all as an unclean thing, and all our righteousness
are as a filthy rag.* (Isaiah 64:6). This time he left a bite mark.
She was found in a little lane, strangled with her nylons, raped and beaten.
The story was beginning to get a little tired. After all, she had a child.
The police were everywhere but she knew she was untouchable.
Let them search and pick up every piece of trash, her discarded
bag, the contents gone with her life, a barely discernible rustle and sigh.


IV    Joanne

Sometimes, she sunbathes in her tights in the small back garden,
the sunlight staining her face. He watches from the kitchen window
with fear and desire. She has two children now. Sometimes, by mistake,
she calls me Patricia, the first one, her first born.


*Tracey Herd*

*Founder of the Calvinist Church of Scotland, John Knox has become associated with sanctimonious morality and rabble-rousing preaching. Biographer James Boswell escaped his own Calvinist upbringing, but not the related guilt, to indulge in pleasures of the flesh.*

## To Be John Knox

was hard in the sixteenth century.
Now all you need is a hipster beard
or centrifugal rhetoric to appear
a force in the world. Or a victim.
Nineteen months in a prison galley
did not arouse the sweet tongue
ladies-in-waiting counted on:
*You are beautiful. Your beauty
won't travel beyond the grave* –
Knox's finest shot at flattery.
There has been flattery: a band,
The John Knox Sex Club, could be
flagged as a tribute act. Scotland
usually sidelines revolutionaries,
continues to give an affirming No
vote to Knox, never a Yes man,
who loved England and prayed
for union. Love was unreciprocal,
unconsummated. But there was
consummation. Cardinal Beaton
had ten children, doubtless virgin
births, before his assassination;
one of Knox's daughters married
a murderer. Knox found it near
impossible to disapprove of death.

There was disapproval: kneeling
for communion; the parroting of
prayer books; Popes pious as
cheeseburgers; dancing; queens –
blame Knox, unlikely therapist
on whom to offload Scottish
niche perennials: difficult-to-like
*wha's like us* brigades, blottoed
sectarians, the misty women
conjuring summer rainclouds
from fish shops in Fife, bullied
adolescents with London accents,
the twenty percent Tory voters –
blame Knox: witty, intransigent
iconoclast. Let's nail accusations
before the High Court carpark.
There he lies beneath berth 23,
powerless under a Mini Clubman.

*Rob A Mackenzie*

# Wee Bozzy Boswell

Wee Bozzy Boswell
rins tae Lunnon Toun,
sooks up tae Sammy –
writes it aw doun;
back in Auld Reekie,
jinks up a close,
gaes wi a hizzie,
gets himsel a dose.

Boozy Bozzy Boswell,
fou as a wulk,
heid like a fitbaw,
gaes hame tae sulk;
awns up tae Margaret
in her nichtgoun,
sets her aff greetin –
writes it aw doun.

Busy Bozzy Boswell,
bleezin wi life,
feart o his faither,
bad tae his wife;
stares at the starnies,
trips ower his shoon,
kisses his bairnies –
writes it aw doun.

Puir Bozzy Boswell,
seik-sair wi sin:
if he wins tae Heaven,
wull they let him in?
Keeks in the mirror –
sic a wickit loun!
Vows tae be a guid man –
writes it aw doun.

Weary Bozzy Boswell,
he pechs and he sighs:
canna help bein Scottish,
hooiver hard he tries.
Ach! Whit a penance!
Och! Whit a boon!
Wee Bozzy Boswell
writes it aw doun.

*James Robertson*

# Thon Place

SULLOM VOE ~ SCAPA FLOW

ARTHUR'S SEAT ~ THE INACCESSIBLE PINNACLE

THE BARRAS ~ JENNERS

THE CALLANISH STONES ~ LITTLE SPARTA

THE CLYDE ~ THE SPEY

SKARA BRAE ~ POLPHAIL

ST KILDA ~ GRUINARD

## SULLOM VOE ~ SCAPA FLOW

*While both are alike in providing their island's focal point, each differs wildly in context. Sullom Voe is Shetland's oil terminal, the landfall for much of North Sea oil; Scapa Flow, once a naval anchorage, is the now peaceful natural harbour at the centre of the scattered islands of Orkney.*

## To Sullom Voe
*for Mary Blance*

From the highest rock at the top of the hill
To the lowest stone in the ebb,

Past Lunna Kirk's old wood pews pipelines
Knit gas to Sullom Voe

Through the islands' simmer dim
Where glaciated grass still swoons,

Rising and birling under a gale
Of unleashed fiddlers' reels that sweep

From the highest rock at the top of the hill
To the lowest stone in the ebb.

*Robert Crawford*

# Scapa Flow, 2016

We squelch on peat and film the stone
as if to catch its crumble into sand.

Tom on the shore lists names for us,
Orphir, Hoy, Houton, The Bu,
plays skimmie-stones, counting six, seven,
young muscles perfect to the task
Grandad taught him.

Once he'd have been spotting
warships. Now it's tourists, divers,
birds calling, flat water.
The tide turns.

He talks about oil and prawns,
spoots and tangle, bere scones.
Grandfather smiles,

undaunted by the dead,
so many, under soil or sea,
properly named. We strain to hear
the sound of skimming stones
and Tom decides
the silent ones are best.
Give and take, the tide runs.

The peace he stands in
not a paper one, a pen
scraping its hasty scrawl.
Quiet as bedrock.
Slow like the making of sand.

*Kate Armstrong*

*From a walk in the park to a serious climb. Dominating the capital city, Arthur's Seat rises to 250m behind Holyrood Palace. At the peak of the second highest of the Cuillins on Skye, The Inaccessible Pinnacle is the most difficult summit of all the Munros.*

## Taking My Mother To Higher Ground

It is not hard to climb, our sleeping lion, its paths
worn and tourist-trodden. I tell her it will take us
half an hour and we will picnic at its summit.

Our lives had been sedentary for so long
before I left her for Scotland that she cannot
fathom a mountain, a thing to climb.

But I want her to see my chosen hometown
in all its glory: castle to crag, palace to firth.
I want her to feel the victory of reaching the peak.

Our ascent is slow with many stops to rest.
She touches the ruined walls of St Anthony's,
takes in the changing cloud-light; I kick away

the broken bottles. She questions my directions,
certain I am taking her somewhere she cannot go.
Volcanic rocks skirt our path, gorse, heather.

My rucksack grows heavier. I talk to fill the hollow
that signposts her tiredness, but do not mention
the tiny coffins found here, or my small anxiety

at her slow speed, now that she's retired to a town
where waves rose so fast, those that couldn't climb
to higher ground died. Instead, we reach the summit,

two hundred and fifty meters high; we share snacks,
cast our eyes as far as we can on a day with no haar.
She seems relieved, or is it pride? She survived.

*Aiko Greig*

# The In Pin

You brand me *Very Difficult*, as if I'm here
to challenge men who fritter days in stuffy

office blocks, evenings in provincial sheds
Sundays crawling up the backs of gods.

You peruse my Munro kin like bridies
on a buffet tray, but I'm the tricky bugger.

I make you strain with ropes. I don't flinch
at your pitons. Gobs gape at my drop,

arseholes pucker tight as drawstring hoods.
I can't be *Bagged* like a tin of shortie

or a bottle of scotch. I've felt the shifting
of tectonic plates, cracked and shuddered

through glacial drift. I've watched clans clash
like stags, flags indecipherable with blood.

Rain will rust your bolts, their fine red dust
tossed by the wind like ashes. You may fancy

your eroding steps superior to any other
Tommy Tourist's, but watch your back.

I'm born of lava: my jutting jaw a blade's edge,
my basalt skull treacherous when wet.

*Jacqueline Thompson*

## THE BARRAS ~ JENNERS

*Known as the 'Harrods of the North', Jenners department store is the haunt of Edinburgh's ladies-of-a-certain-age – and class. The Barras street market in Glasgow's East End is famous as the place to nab almost any sort of purchase – at a bargain price.*

## The Barras

At the fag-end of afternoon – the sky a yawn
behind dark buildings, stalls half-dismantled –
cheap cardis, limp oversized tee-shirts
fail to convince, stage-props after the last
curtain. Under this sprawl of East End streets
the centuries jostle, stacked like pauper coffins.

Do you hear street-cries – a fish wife's screech
out of the Briggait, a wide boy's weegie patter,
accents from Irish to Punjabi? In the blurred light
a few late punters morph into brylcreemed hopefuls
queuing for Barrowlands, shopgirls in quest
of bargain glamour. This place trades on illusion

like Glasgow herself, raddled beauty
with Tennents breath, getting her gladrags on
for a night on the lash, a dab of fake Chanel
behind her ears, the jewels in her hair
winking so brightly that we never ask
whether they are diamond or glass.

*A C Clarke*

# Caryatid

*Because Symbolically Women are the Support of the House – Charles Jenner*

When I dream about slim-line peppermints
it is because I want to be a bird, and when
I want to be a bird, I really want to be a flock
of birds silhouetted on a tablemat, and when
my wings get sticky from ox-tongue soup
and marmalade, a hand will come to wipe
them clean with a sponge that tastes of meat.
And when I dream about meat, it is because
I want to be a woman, and when I want to be
a woman, I really want to be a woman
carved in stone, with stone bones, stone hair
and a stone bow and arrow. And I will stand
as a buttress on the old department store
and never doubt that I am hefty and angelic.

But when I dream about never doubting
it is because I want to get lost, and when
I want to get lost, I really want to get lost
in a little curtained cubicle, full of coat-hangers
and clumps of dust, and squares of coloured silk.
Of course this is not glorious or realistic enough
just as measuring spoons are not glorious enough
and nor are faux leather pine cones, or abstract pears
on coasters. But when I dream about abstract
pears on coasters, it is because I want domestic bliss
and when I want domestic bliss all I want
is to stop pushing cupboards against insufficient
doors, and peeling snails off PVC nasturtiums.

*Tessa Berring*

THE CALLANISH STONES ~ LITTLE SPARTA

*Ian Hamilton Finlay created Little Sparta over 40 years. The Lanarkshire garden is a fusion of poetic and sculptural elements in over 275 works. The Callanish Stones were erected 5,000 years ago on the Isle of Lewis by unknowable Neolithic architects.*

## The Callanish Stones

July. Summer on the island
muffles in scarves.
Merino-socked, Berghaus-booted,

swap cocoon of car
for hilly slither. Pilgrim-trail
with sodden strangers,

step in time to the cadence of rain.
White-trainered Americans patter: *there isn't a bus,*
*Earl, I can't believe there isn't a bus.*

Even taped seams leak. Cold
as Lewisian gneiss, circle
the circle of Neolithic ritual.

Reach out, for Callanish grants
what Stonehenge forbids:
it feels like wet stone.

On the downhill squelch,
the final syllable's a sneeze.
I buy a fridge magnet.

*Nikki Robson*

# Little Sparta

 thistles first
    on the path
        to the long gate

opening
    the enclosed space
        anthology of dug and planted

words on stone
    stones on grass
        boat on water

gods abound
    but the greatest
        is paronomasia

nature/nurture
    decide/decode
        it's all translation

in this Arcadia
    the bird table
        is an aircraft carrier

(though the whirly's
    a whirly
        hanging

with abandoned clothespegs
    and there's kail
        in the kailyard)

an epicure's delight
    pure dead
        brilliant

ultimately dissolving
    in the noise
        of tree shells

or is it the hiss
    of the guillotine's
        blade?

in a field beyond the fence
    there's a crow
        in a cage

*Hamish Whyte*

THE CLYDE ~ THE SPEY

*The waterway of Clut or the River Clyde was the centre of the ancient Kingdom of Strathclyde becoming the cradle of the Industrial Revolution in Scotland. The River Spey, in Gaelic Uisge Spè, is central to whisky distilling, salmon fishing and tourism.*

# Headwaters

My blood is in the Clyde.
A broken bottle in the burn –
threads pulsing out under the viaduct
and westwards. *The Clyde will be changing
colour tomorrow,* my father said. *Red Clydeside.*
Binding my foot tighter in his handkerchief
to carry me back to his mother's house.
        I used to swim here as a boy, the water
        was darker then.

A rusting cast-iron tub released from
its hungry thirties, weekly washhouse stint
now rested at the end of my granny's garden
concocting its potent liquid manure from
tattie shaws, nettles, all manner of peelings,
peapods and sulphurous Lanarkshire rain
which would leach any goodness into the river
        unless she caught it for the clay she turned
        in old pit boots – for her tatties and kail.

Remembering her eldest travelling the line
north of the river towards St Mary's High,
Whifflet ('the little whiff') by Coatbridge –
so much schoolboy brightness borne
into the daily smoking darkness mined
by men like his dad, two years killed,
for men like him and me –
        the cinder trail, the magnate's metronome,
        our rattling train at dawn for Glasgow Central.

That brassy taste of 1950s smogs.
Staring to make out through mirk
the numbers on trams we could hear
but not see yet, I was scared of getting
doubly lost. We wore handkerchiefs
across our faces like sooty bandits.
And back at the ranch at last
        blowing your nose was a Whistlerian
        study in black on white.

Now Clydeside's a postcard. Of pensioners
posing for snaps on the Rothesay Ferry –
an outing long before that word got gay
and proud. Stout women in herringbone coats
buttoned up to their knitted sou'westers
like mermaids in glasses
or barnacled goddesses staring
        out from the prow into what's left
        of the teeth of life's gale.


*James McGonigal*

# Spey

Spey runs to Tay runs into Liffey
Becomes Vltava.

I knew a man that saw the Spey and drank it.
When he woke up, it was in Turkey.
A flying carpet brought him home.
I looked for him in Warriston
But did not see him there.

Spey runs to Tay runs into Liffey
Becomes Vltava.

I was not told and did not ask.
The bodies on the Stony Beach was all I knew.
A stag in the water at Mugdrum.
The Dundee Dry Dock instead of Sunday school.
And Liffey (now I'm Irish) was never far to swim.

Spey runs to Tay runs into Liffey
Becomes Vltava.

My boy knows the river and its castles.
At Zvikov once he broke an axe.
In Krumlov he fought Germans.
Above the gates of Prague,
He holds the hands of ghosts.

Spey runs to Tay runs into Liffey
Becomes Vltava.

I will see the Spey again and when I do
Beharrie will be waiting.
Stuarts, Jacks and Christies will smile at me
From stones langsyne laid
At Dallas and Aberlour.

*Matthew Fitt*

SKARA BRAE ~ POLPHAIL

*Two abandoned settlements of very different eras. One is a cluster of Orcadian dwellings from the Stone Age, hidden from view for 5,000 years, the other a derelict 'ghost village' (now demolished) built to house oil workers for a 1970s West Coast boom that never materialised.*

## Skara Brae

Trace the passage of planets and stars
scratched with talons of scavengers
on to the corridor walls as you creep

past the doors of the old, snecked
against darkness and cold. Bow
low as though crossing the threshold

to kindle the fire in the home
of your soul. Don't stand in the shadows,
filling that dresser with bric-a-brac,

betting slips, black and white photos
of family fishing trips; measuring beds
for duvets and memory foam mattresses.

You won't make it your own without limpets
softening in troughs, an axe in each alcove,
ancestors under your feet.  Don't envy

our diet of venison, barley and lobster –
henbane's not optional, living half-buried
in midden material. And though everything's set

in stone, this is not Scotland – just water and sand
where survival's an accident
waiting to happen.

*Lindsay Macgregor*

# Polphail Village

*I have long had this premonition*
*of a bright day and a deserted house.*

    – Anna Akhmatova


Only the bodies of birds, bats and sheep
inhabit this place

so when we come here, we become bird-like,
bat-like, sheep-like.

Everything is transformed –
washing machine drums have become eyes;

a cairn of stones – a small body
curled in the corner of a muddy couch.

We taste brick dust, wet fur, sea air
on our tongues.

It's the first day of New Year
and somehow my body feels as unlived-in

and crumbling as the houses
breaking around us.

How they speak to us – the door
hanging off its hinges; the emerald

puddle of algae in the bathtub;
glass shattering under our boots.

A flight of stairs step off mid-air
to somewhere we cannot follow.

Here, walls sprout words, pictures,
the enormous face of a woman –

her gold-touched eyes watching
from a distance.

The hardened spines of winter gorse
are closing in, the tarmacked ground fractured;

its cracks matching the heart line,
head line and life line on my left hand.

We walk through the Polphail inside of us –
smashed up houses, writing on the wall.

They call it a ghost village
but there are no ghosts here, simply

another expression of ourselves.

*Marion McCready*

ST KILDA ~ GRUINARD

*Almost as famous for its abandonment, St Kilda was, until 1930, the most remote inhabited island in the UK. The once-populated island of Gruinard was requisitioned in 1942 for the testing of germ warfare agents and rendered uninhabitable as a consequence.*

## Guth ri Ràdh

Ghlaoidheadh iad a-mach ann an Hiort:
*Tha Goill air a' Ghleann!*
Agus thug iad an cnatan-mòr a-steach.

Agus nuair a dh'èirich a leithid dhaibh
Gus nach blaiseadh iad am beathachadh
Is nach fhaigheadh iad fàileadh ann

Is nach fhaiceadh is nach dùisgeadh ach air èiginn
Is nach cluinneadh is nan cante: *Ciamar a tha sibh
A' faireachdainn?* 's gun canadh iad, mar a thuirt

Agus am bodach eile: *Och, guth ri ràdh!*
'S e na dh'fhairich iad an uair sin
Ann an da-rìribh: *Tha, dìreach a' bàsachadh.*

*Rody Gorman*

# Nothing To Be Said

They'd cry out in the village in St Kilda:
*There are foreigners in the glen!*
And they brought in the influenza.

And after they contracted it
And could no longer taste their food –
Fulmar, gannet, puffin – or smell anything

And couldn't speak and couldn't wake, even,
And couldn't hear and if you asked
*And how are you feeling?*

And they'd say like they did
*Och, nothing to be said!*
Actually, *Dying* is what they really meant.

*Rody Gorman*

# Gruinard Island

*what is the manner of sacrifice*
a lamb born with blood on its ears
from a heaving heft-over ewe mother
born purple and yellow of caul
a suckling lamb nuzzling

what's the nature of an offering
a tethered mother a ewe
in her body panting after labour
tonguing uterus blood lamb and faeces
we'll gralloch her flense her

*without the shedding of blood*
*there is no forgiveness*
twelve times seven ewes
on a rock in the sea
hooded and tethered seven days

exploded from the gallows
Bacillus anthracis entering ewe breath
we'll paunch and slice
a rite of our terror-dread
smear and smother bomb

four pound bombs in clusters
of one hundred and six
in two thousand seven hundred aircraft
each with forty thousand charnel-clusters of toxin
our benefaction to burn three million in six cities

*how pleasing the aroma*
each first lamb to each last lamb
each first bullock to each last bullock
each first born to each last born
each first nation to each last nation

burning

    *Gerry Loose*

# Bill o Fare

ENA BAXTER ~ TONY SINGH

LAPHROAIG ~ BUCKFAST

CULLEN SKINK ~ IRN BRU

ARBROATH SMOKIE ~ EDINBURGH ROCK

More identified with a predilection for traditional 'plain food', Ena Baxter was the doyenne of Baxters of Speyside. But tastes change. Here Tony Singh, the TV chef and inventor of the haggis pakora, meets the creator of Royal Game soup.

## Ena Baxter Soup

*As Gordon Baxter was fond of saying: 'Where's Mrs Heinz? Collecting French Impressionists…Where's Mrs Baxter? In the kitchen making soup!'*
    – Obituary: *Ena Baxter, Soup Entrepreneur*, The Telegraph, 20 January 2015

Take a douce childhood on a couthy Huntly farm,
a mouth for a good recipe,
the perseverance of Greer Garson's Marie Curie,
a husband who's a son of Moray and has a canning factory,
game from the hill, fish from the burn,
an artist's eye,
and a stockpot.

Leave the teaching of art. Pick up a wooden spoon.
Invent Baxter's Chicken Gumbo Soup.
Sell a million cans in the first year.
Move on to Royal Game, Scotch Broth, Cock-a-Leekie,
the Lobster Bisque that's kept for best,
the Cullen Skink Prince Philip likes.
Much more than just a tin of soup.

Don't stop there, work on the marmalades and jams.
Pioneer the twist top jar.
Pickle beetroot, can haggis, preserve pheasant in wine jelly.
Send Scotland to Japan, Korea, and the USA.
Appear on TV in a pinny.
Be seen in the kitchen with the stockpot, the secret recipes,
not at all like Mrs Heinz.

Write a Scottish Cookbook for industrious housewives.
Feature on the cover having a picnic in your kilt.
Explain how to salt a herring and sew up a haggis.
Remind us of the wholesome food we didn't used to like:
Feather Fowlie, Powsowdie, Hough Soup,
Mealy Pudding, Clapshot, Clootie Dumpling.
Just don't mention opening a tin.

Keep it in the family. When the time is right,
hand over to Audrey.
Pick up your paint brushes.

*Elspeth McLean*

## Masala

Leith's infused in spice, cracked pepper
terraces, knock-off shops, bric-a-bracs,
renovations simmering along its waterside.

In caboodled Caledonian kitchens
rubia turbans sing and sizzle, wet summer
fruits jam for the right caster and seasons.
A lick will bring the blood to boil; veins
pulsed from the nuptial pots of Delhi
to stalwart queues in Scottish diners.

Picture a bowl: snaw-white, braw
by the pound of spice snoozing in its belly.
Think mulligatawny, kedgeree, tikka masala,
haggis pakora (with chips?) and the steam
of history engulfs the room. Tear the morning
roll, naan, Mother's Pride – it's not just the dish
that makes the meal, but the appetite.

*Russell Jones*

LAPHROAIG ~ BUCKFAST

*Few stereotypes are as fixed as the Scottish drunk, but here viewed from opposite social extremes. Islay single malt Laphroaig is 'the most medicinal of Scotches', while Buckfast, a tonic wine made by monks, is much associated with antisocial behaviour.*

## Uisge Beatha

Gies a gless o yon amber swahly, ice-chinklin,
skinklin at the rim, reekin o an Islay boanfire;
a bouquet o burnt tehr an a ticky sugarelly watter
peat-steepit in tar an iodine.

Pass owre a tummlerfuhl o the cauld, wild west,
mahltit barley, slow-distilt, pure poetrie;
thon lang eftertist, heather colloguin wi dulse,
a douce toffee-aipple, a smoky baccy guff;
tert an sweet, smooth an smartin, mallayin the tongue,
sic a brah Manichaean dichotomie!

Gies a wee nip o the gowden meld, huggit lang-time in sherried oak.
Poor oot a dram ti weet wir thrapple, prickle wir palate,
gie thae tistbuds a helluva fleg, birl them, mak them dirl.

Shove yir cognac wi its pinkie in the air, kiddin-on it's pedigree.
Stuff yir peely-wally reamin swats o barley bree.
Awa wi yir Ruski voddie's stringent ming o fermentin tattie.
Ruby rum's wahrm an reekin-rich bit
thir's nae dusky musk ... nae *je ne sais quoi*.

Dinna feel guilt fir a meenit, dinna think yir wrang.
Angels aa share it wi'oot a secint thocht.
Dinna skimp noo, nae grippit huddin-back; dinna be ticht-fistit.
Heelstergowdie in luv wi feisty Laphroaig,
wi'll sip, syne swig an drap doon inti yon mella dwam.

Poor yirsel an uisge beatha, wrap roond it, real slow,
drink in its mony colours, droon in its pungent glow.

*Fran Baillie*

## Commotion Lotion

*[…] politicians, the* BBC *and a bishop say consumers may be hyperactive, incoherent and rather violent.*
— The Daily Mail

Ma burd is eywis dancin
an it wudnae be a bad hing
but ah don't get nae luvvin
an thats nae lie.
We spent the night in Costco
instead ay at the disco,
an fae tha night ah kissed wur luv goodbye.

Don't blame it oan the sunburn
Don't blame it oan the hen night
Don't blame it oan the coke-line
Blame it oan the Buckie.

The nasty Buckie bugs hur
– jist somehoo grabs an mugs hur
hur spellboond gluggin tips hur off hur feet.
It's changed wur life completely
ah've had ma tastebuds leave me
I never swallyd onyhin so sweet.

Don't blame it oan the shoeshine
Don't blame it oan the munter
Don't blame it oan the greetin
Blame it oan the Buckie.

It looks a loat like Bisto
wi a nose like Eric Bristow
and a fust like Benny Lynch, like, oan a Satdy night.
Ma burd, she tans a botil
an passes oot in Lidl
but nae afore she's goat intae a fight.

Don't blame it oan the banter
Don't blame it oan the stoater
Don't blame it oan the cargo
Blame it oan the Buckie.

Pure canny
pure canny
pure canny control ma burd
pure canny
pure canny
canny hawd ma hoachin burd.

Ma skank's a steamin jakey,
she doons a few then skelps me
reelly rips ma knittin hoo she's oot hur heid.
Ef any bam says 'pie it,'
or 'hairy, ye should diet,'
she malkies him, then chibs him, an he's deid.

Don't blame it oan the monkies
Don't blame it oan the Abbey
Don't blame it oan the polis
Blame it oan the Buckie.

*Claudia Daventry*

## IRN BRU ~ CULLEN SKINK

*From the nip to the swallie, from broth to brose, liquid refreshment goes down a treat in Scotland. Almost as iconic as whisky, Irn-Bru is our 'other national drink' while Cullen Skink, a soup of smoked haddie, tatties and ingans, has become a national classic.*

## The Declaration of Barrbru

```
        a       co l  d
m     i  s  t
            c  l              i
       n                  g       s
                    from
              o l   d           der
                t           i de s,
    a      s
                    d r       e
    a                   m       s
          co l
                l             i de:
                c       r       e
    a           t             e
    a
                        f     i    er
              c                     er
m     e           an        i
         n                  g.
                    from
m     i         d         de
          n
                    t     o
ma        n s                  e,
```

```
            s
        i   c
    a
      d   in
    a     n
       e  n    t
                    fr      e
        e       d   om;
                    f
    a       l           s
      e
                la        ird  s
                  and f
                la
                   t
          i         d         e
    a    s.
             s o
           i  s  land      ers
      de    c          i de:
      de    s   t         i
            n             i  e
          i  s
                    o    r
    a    n              g   e.
   ma    n     and
   m    i        d      g   e,
            n   ot
   made      t      o
                       o    rder:
   made in Scotland from girders.
```

*Rebecca Sharp*

## Cullen Skink

*The Cullen Skink World Championship*
*has commenced and the battle for the crown –*
*contested by more than a dozen hopefuls – is hotting up!*

Ye swither atween the deil o a broth
and a deep sea stew o tatties, ingans,
a drappie milk and scraps o smuikit haddie.

And whit a braw and couthie appellation
that tickles outrels and, in locals forby,
boosts pride in thir ain hame-branded cuisine!

    Oh skink, oh skink, oh cullen skink,
    I love yir skinkle, yir neb-twitchin stink.

On tartanned tables o Balmoral Hotels
fae Edina tae Durban yi scrub up fair perjink,
wi chiffonades o parsley, drizzles o cream

but forget yir airs and graces. Dae yir job.
Cheer the hert and warm the painch o shilpit folk.
Ye wir aye humble fare. And nane the waur o it.

*Dilys Rose*

ARBROATH SMOKIE ~ EDINBURGH ROCK

*The Arbroath Smokie, salted haddock smoked over a fire of beech and oak, is made using methods dating back to the late 1800s. Edinburgh Rock, a traditional Scottish confection, was first made in the 19th century. Both remain popular to this day.*

## The Numbers Stations

We were like fish out of water in those days,
hanging about in pairs at the back of the bike shed
on Keptie Road with a shared Number 6, nursing

the latest rumours of World War Three. First clue:
that woman knee-deep in the Short Wave slush
singing *The Auchmithie Fishwife* backwards.

Later, Badgers grumbling over from Murmansk
with their cargo of megatons; Leuchars snuffed out
in a blink, the Bell Rock's candle lit one final time

as the blast wave rushes out like a single ripple
across a pond, searing the Strath as far as Fettercairn.
We would all be saved, of course, by the bike shed's

blue asbestos walls. Trailing home, days later,
here's me coming upon my Father in the garden pond,
smoke-grey rucks of skin sloughing from his flesh

and the cured flesh peeling easily from the bone
and every bone burned clean of whatever let it move,
but still he's lingering on; his hand held out for mine.

*John Glenday*

# Edinburgh Castle Rock

the four of us pressed round the click
of our five sticks of cellophaned rock
still boxed inside the castle's cardboard neb
& splash of sugared tartan
                       & how
we'd squabble for our favourite colour
snatch untwist the shiny crack the stick
to chumble in the teeth as sweet
as pop a holiday treat
                       & tear
down the street a yelping clan o still
those red clay pantiles sunlit in my head
Crail's beach that *beggar's mantle*
*fringed wi gowd* would open wide
                       & there
we'd let the rock melt on
our tongues like honeyed chalk
& singalong and play
team games
                       led on
by Christians on the make
who'd mind us bairns
& bleach us souls
& give our mum a break

*Jean Atkin*

# Gaun Aboot

THE GLASGOW SUBWAY ~ THE VITAL SPARK

JOHN O'GROATS ~ LOCH LOMOND

THE BRIDGE OVER THE ATLANTIC ~ THE FORTH BRIDGE

SAUCHIEHALL STREET ~ THE ROYAL MILE

THE GLASGOW SUBWAY~ THE VITAL SPARK

*The Glasgow Subway – nicknamed 'The Clockwork Orange' – consists of just one route around the city centre. In contrast are the fictional stravaigings of The Vital Spark, captained by Para Handy, whose adventures first appeared in print in 1905.*

## The Clockwork Orange

Our most frequented stretch: Hillhead to Buchanan Street
or burrowing under the Clyde, after the Citz, the tunnel
walls streaming, rats scuttling, stations knee-deep in litter,
each arrival announced by a rumble and gust of sour air.
Yet the Clockwork Orange secure in our affections: we'd
vouch visitors a treat on our state-of-the-art Subway Circle

then note their shock (though its cable days long gone)
at the ill-lit entrance, toy-town rolling-stock; debouching
from shoogly carriages, through clattering gates
on to a narrow platform; hauling cases up the steps,
not an escalator in sight – unsure whether to believe
they could buy the unique aroma, bottled, as a souvenir.

Hard, given my absence, to credit today's streamlined
version, carmine-and-cream livery, contoured sliding
doors. For all its elegance and speed, *la nostalgie de la boue*
prevails: as though on archival film, two fur-coated ladies
emerge, turn left, and a bauchle in a green uniform bawls:
*Hey missis, for tae get oot that wey youse'll need a pick and shovel*

    *Stewart Conn*

# The Vital Spark

*for Bert Arnott*

Which long forgotten birthday did it mark
That match-less model of The Vital Spark
Run aground on a Glasgow bathroom shelf?
My friend, an Inveraray man himself

Knew well, such vintage vessels' lure for me
Whose laid-off father ran away to sea
Cruising river, estuary, and loch
*Puffer, puffer, puffer*: making steam talk

Like that other engineer, and Dan, MacPhail
Two cylinders, coal fired, a pier-less, sail
Boat, *fully laden, our famed, shallow draft*
*Navigates straits too dire for larger craft*

Inlets, isles, kyles, canals, the wild west coast
The time served tool-maker's, mariner's, boast
That he never went under, just below
Saved from the Depression by Neil Munro

Who gathered those stories in 'thirty one
When Dad made a glorified gabbert run.
In gansey, oilskin, cap and rubber boots
Dan plied the coastal trade's old birlinn routes

*On a cut off islet, girls' grateful cries*
*When we came ashore with a month's supplies.*
Or was it the 'Maggie' that eased folk's plight?
Ealing's changed names, pirating copyright

To watch with father was to hear him state
The need to recognise, Dougie, The Mate
(Hugh Foulis's fables were *nom de plumed*
TV identities went un-assumed)

On BBC Sundays, we'd stow away
Skipper MacMillan relieving MacRae
Dad's spell aboard, though brief, deemed, 'chust sublime'
Couthy capers recalled the maritime

The youthful stand-in logged each mythic trip
Chapter closed; time to tie up plot, and ship
War found factory berths for engineers
Boiler rooms foresworn for fifty fond years

Wheelhouse, hold, funnel, derrick, single mast
Stove, bluff bow, captain's cabin, aft… Things past
Till being towed downstream for scrap, Dan saw
Her forlorn fo'c'sle leave The Broomielaw

Whimsical, pawky, sentimental, fey
The half true romance, *Gael* yard tales convey
Tonight on Clyde-Side, with every wave
The Para Handy's crew and I still crave

A twilight ceilidh, across sparkling seas
A last, wistful waltz, in the Hebrides
Where Sunny Jim's melodeon will play
The day that puffer carries me away

Scaled down. Not diminished. Oceanless. There.
Dream boat, Atlantic breakers shan't deter
If the clapped out engines pass the chief's test
We will both set out on the voyage west

*Donny O'Rourke*

JOHN O'GROATS ~ LOCH LOMOND

*Two attractions on every tourist's itinerary. John O'Groats is not the country's most northerly point but it is far too late to change that general perception now. Loch Lomond suffers from a similar misconception, being named after the mountain rather than vice versa.*

## John O'Groats

Endings are not entirely bitter: here,
where the land gives out
in a last flourish of sea-pink, sand
and louring cliff,
the Atlantic and North Sea
join to sing, sometimes in a mother's croon,
often with the battle cry of a marauder.

Sky is everywhere you look: underneath it
coastal townships busy themselves
with a million small inconsequentialities.
Stacked one upon the other,
all these particulars conspire to build
the shaky watchtowers we all gaze from.

Air is sharp and vital, cut with salt,
seasoned with a blend
of moorland bloom and arctic ice.
Conversation, cautious but frank, reflects
a recognition that each wave and every breeze,
each shaft of autumn sunlight
unfolds depending only on its inner strength.

Balanced on the outer edge,
we watch each moment spool before our eyes,
knowing the future is uncharted sea,
certain there is no way back to land.

*Ian McDonough*

# Mobarik Picnic

I

The Knot

At Loch Lomond they were king and queen to me,
laying out their bounty on the brae
after the queasy ride from Glasgow, we
children making sick-stops on the way.

Tumbled out, we sprawled at the water's mouth
where light ate shade and made us ravenous.
With a flourish, Her Majesty untied the cloth
to set parathas free. She did, she does,

undoes this deep red knot of hurt in the heart.
Today, when scars have been allowed to deepen
around a silence, wrenching our lives apart,
she has come back to us at the loch to open

out the tangle of her dying, the mistake,
the high, the low, the road we did not take.

II

## Chaudhri Sher Mobarik Looks at the Loch

Light shakes out the dishrag sky
and scatters the water with sequins. *Look, hen!*
says my father, *Loch Lomond!* as if
it were all his doing, as if he owned it,
laird of Lomond, laird of the language.
He is proud to say hen and even more loch
with an och not an ock, to speak
proper Glaswegian like a true-born Scot,
and he makes the right sound at the back
of the throat because he can say khush
and khwab and khamosh, because the sounds
for happy and dream are the words that swim
in the water for him, so he says it again,
*Hen! Look! The loch!*

*Imtiaz Dharker*

# SAUCHIEHALL STREET ~ THE ROYAL MILE

*Two great thoroughfares provide a window on the extremes of urban Scotland. The Royal Mile, Edinburgh's tourist promenade stretches from Holyrood Palace to the Castle. Glasgow's main drag, Sauchiehall Street, is more the haunt of locals on a shopping spree or a night out.*

## Sauchiehall Street

Sauchiehall Street is space-blue and silver in winter
her alien-hex skin pressed with diamonds and dust, her slick vertebrae
make way for the applaud of cars where a therapy of ignition tracks
      her spine
to spill champagne and socialists, tranquilise pedestrians, run ladders
      in pre-war stockings.

In summer she gives you that look like someone horn-struck
and about to undress in front of you, so you blank out all the side-streets
concentrate on her striptease breaching dilated pupils – on those nights
      she reaches for lovers,
seduces them under her skirt of shuttered shops; velvet saunas, skyscraper
      hotels, cocktail hours.

This street is more hysterical than historical, as most women tend to be
      marked,
her lips too numb for kisses, so she spits into the mouth of pollution,
      swallows traffic cones.

When bleached by the gulf of self-loathing she lets knives flash under her
      street-lamps,
bends to gear violence into her palm like loosened fruit still sore from its
      secular branch-snap
prone to flex post-mortem.

She hoards the hooligans in their hoods, samples a taste of their furious
    hunger,
holds them the same way stags grip those wretched birds of paradise in
    their midnight antlers.

Oh Sauchiehall Street you are a hall of mirrors with your music-hall name
    delivering illusion
Glasgow's graceless steps palpitate towards stampede to unhinge your
    promised land,
shadows display a promenade of romances on The Locarno Ballroom
    dance floor.

The sad bottled eyes of French girls in polyester on their way to
    Kelvingrove
awake in clusters with their faces creased like abandoned linen
    dizzy from the smell of cordite in their dreams.

This street is not a language or a place to salvage euphoria,
oh no, there is a helpful smile in every aisle if you trust the magician's saw
and newsreaders on every corner to renegade tomorrow's cry of surrogate
    heroes.

Her sign posts promote neutrality to scaffold the future, because despite
    bomb blasts
Mackintosh still coloured tearooms with stained glass and Art Deco
    reigned
over posh shops, luncheon frills, high-end theatres where Sinatra sang

those years after open-air suffragettes paraded taffeta and no surrender
or cadmium orange tramcars ivory trim with plum dashes pulsed over
    cobbles –
the internal grits and gifts of life, a gold-gilded cinema-mad city,
    smokeless, slow. Burning.

*Janette Ayachi*

# The Royal Mile

Volcanic jizz on a world tour
found its sweet spot of latitude
and got embedded, crag and tail.
In due course history, fortress
down to palace – pecking orders
and disorders, death and soirées,
epiphanies, piss on cobbles,
persistence of the hellfire gene.
And here they came in cavalcades
we'd see the bill for later on –
the royal actors, performing
those slow waves, top of the bill,
off to stain a stage somewhere
maybe with their blood, more likely ours.

But where I'd barge to the tryline
there's that Parliament we built;
The People's Story cleared a space
for some tartan tins that shipped
Father's shortbread recipes
to the high teas of the world;
just across the road, my books
in the Scottish Poetry Library
sit where the crack is sparkiest;
and down here, love, is where we used
to browse and buy all the maps
of where we'd been and wouldn't get to.

Read the signs there: Paterson's Land.
And that's true. It's my mile too.

*Alasdair Paterson*

THE BRIDGE OVER THE ATLANTIC ~ THE FORTH BRIDGE

*An 'icon' of Scotland, The Forth Bridge opened in 1890 and is acknowledged as one of the wonders of the modern world. The ironically named 'Bridge Over the Atlantic' links, in a single span, the island of Seil to the Argyll mainland, crossing an inlet of the ocean as it does.*

## The Bridge Over The Atlantic

They took our birlinn, stem and stern-posts
High as a Venetian gondola's, and up-turned it.
Every tide in the bladder-wracked sea-tongue its keel

Bridged, swam the eel-current
Races that tracked South and North
Into and out of the Atlantic. And they
Docked our tongues, every man's that dared
Give out a taste of his father's banter,
Effortless sound-shapes an islander's born to.

One soul this end of the keel-bridge, one the other;
Veritable shape-shifters we were, minds gone
Evasive as mist with keeping speech-thoughts in curb,
Raking the past for the fuelling of anger.

Those that got out, the salmon-stubborn, ran
Hard-headed on a spring ebb out to sea;
Everything given up but nothing given over.

And from Mull and Seil, Caithness and Ireland, Sweden and Italy
The disinherited massed in a marvellous Sargasso;
Language, labour, dance of the old worlds gathered
And ransacked the past for ways of living
New. New? For our first night we took a skin canoe,
Tipped its fur-clad family into Scajaquada Creek, then
Inverted it. We wound their heathen souls in a keening
Calliach's plaid of consonants and vowels.

*Ian Crockatt*

# Forth Bridge Calligramme

                                                Watanabe                                        Arrol's wark
                                   Fowler       Baker                                tae marshal it
                  the engineers   showin us    hou it's daen               tons o steel
          in defiance o      fear      guid sense      gravity     o whilk the hinmaist   - gowd -

## The wonder: hou the trains gang

    the North shore    aa the weys    ye kin fail    kin tummle    haunt ye      caissons   fir the deep foondati
whaur the forces anchor      the locomotive   droon'd    deep i the Tay        caissons
          coal country        the architect    deid o shame         an the ae caisson
  industry in thir bones      or onywey that's the story               months' chauvi

THE BRIDGE OVER THE ATLANTIC ~ THE FORTH BRIDGE

                                    a century an a hauf
        fifty thoosand                      inspection        maintenance
six an a hauf    million rivets          the legendary    paint job      niverendin
     sunk    by the Prince o Wales    strippit back    new coatin    aye    state of the art

horough it ilka day, takin it as a given

     keepin oot    the deep water      the official tally    fifty-seven men    deid    buildin this brig    the Sooth shore
disease o    decompression              historians speak o    mebbe anither    forty forbye    whaur the forces anchor
    skew an foonert                          the uncoonted         sick              reason
  tae richt it                                    an maimed                     Enlichtenment an its science

*Judith Taylor*

THE BRIDGE OVER THE ATLANTIC ~ THE FORTH BRIDGE

# The Gemm

GEORGE KIDD ~ KEN BUCHANAN

ANDREW WATSON ~ ERIC LIDDELL

BILLY BREMNER ~ ARCHIE GEMMILL

BILL McLAREN ~ ARTHUR MONTFORD

*Two masters of the square ring: George Kidd, Dundee's 'Houdini of the Mat', wowed wrestling audiences during that sport's 1960s golden age, while Edinburgh's 'Fighting Carpenter', Ken Buchanan, was surely Scotland's greatest-ever boxer.*

# George Kidd

Bull's blood and vinegar lugs
has it really been so long since you were home
a moth that traveled between towns
flew to occupied countries
cooled and condensed in their archways;
to start they called you Titch

Until the day you double hooked one bully's legs
and squeezed
found a world inside
not even light could escape without bending

Chased Rudi Quarez over continents and the Press
but the body remembers its shapes
and drawn to neon
you top-billed bingo halls
picked out in buzzing bulbs outside – George Kidd.
I'm ten years old.

Come in, submit
it's filling up
beneath the glare from too-bright lights
a whorl of reek punches out dark shapes
gran's powerful French almond scent
tussles with sawdust and iron shavings,

the smell of artificial light on upholstery
a musk of neoprene and Brylcreem.
You took it all lying down
wrist lock chin lock whip, half nelson.

So arrogant he wouldn't raise his hands
Jackie Pallo deckchaired
in that reverse surfboard
winking
like kites in leafless trees, and frieze
rest hold for the camera's
release.

*Richard Watt*

# Ken Buchanan (1945–)
*World Lightweight Champion 1970–1972*

Catch it on YouTube
not just the thirteenth round
but the whole fight
and it's the whole fight
you must watch to feel
even after all these years
breathless
as Roberto
*Hands of Stone* Duran
plunders the space
between them. *Hombre,*
*where you are, there I'll be*
*and nothing will deny me.*
Upright, elegant
the Champion jabs
but can't find the range
for his punches to do
damage. Still, he's in there
with a chance
with *his* heart
always with a chance.

Till at the end of the thirteenth
after the bell Duran swings one
that lands low on Buchanan's
proud tartan shorts
denting his protector –
*Manos de Piedra.*
He shuts like a knife
and goes down.

Even after all this time
it seems impossible
that the referee would then –
the Champion unable to continue –
award the fight to Duran, *Now the new*

*World Lightweight Champion!*
After all this is not a dodgy off-side,
a trip or a dive; this is two men
in Madison Square Gardens
floodlit on a stage before
thousands there, millions at home,
and a blatant punch *after the bell* to
*Ma baws, ma fuckin baws!*

Duran will not honour him
with a re-match –
he doesn't need *him*
to make his millions.
So it seems clear
the gods have stopped
smiling on him and
after a couple of setbacks more
he goes back to being
a joiner. He still loves
the smell of sawdust
and fresh cut wood,
likes being known
simply as 'Ken'.
But he can't let go
of the memory, of how
he was cheated. He just can't
let it lie. He leaves his tools
and flies to New York.
For two weeks he scours
Harlem for Duran, a showdown
on his mind. Always
he has loved to scrap.
A *white* man in Harlem! they say.
But he fears nothing –
for some know him
even there. And who hasn't
wanted to go back
to the place
where you felt your life
unravel? Who hasn't walked

empty streets wanting
one last lover's embrace
or one last tilt
at justice? With what
will the hollowing out
ever be filled?

My daughter, taking the bus
from Edinburgh to Glasgow,
finds herself next to
an older gentleman –
camel coat, be-ringed fingers.
They're both late for meetings,
he for one about...
*Boxing, I'm sorry, I know nothing...*
*Your dad'll have heard of me,*
he tells her and gives her
a signed postcard
of a young boxer –
the gloves up, the body
honed, the face
intense, close to being
pretty, but for the slight
spread of the broken nose.
Below his name
in a shaky hand
he writes *World Champ. Aye,*
he says, *they named*
*this bus station* eftir me.

    Tom Pow

*In 2000, Ken Buchanan MBE was inducted into the International*
*and World Halls of Fame – the only British boxer to win both awards.*

ANDREW WATSON ~ ERIC LIDDELL

*Sport generates unlikely heroes, some of whom posterity restores to greatness. Eric Liddell put God before his sport at the 1924 Olympics but still won 400 metres Gold. In the 1880s Andrew Watson became the first black footballer to play for his country.*

## Unner the Fold

In the sports section, twa paragraphs
unner the fold, an oot o the spotlicht,
I saw a photograph o a toosled chiel
impassive, beckonin me tae find him
beyond the January transfer windae

proodly displayin his country's badge
oan a jersey o pink an yellow bands,
no in a puffed oot boastin way, no
in a hunkered doon ashamed way,
but as it shid be, ain o his nation's best;

a nippy ain tae, wi a hint o Jinky's weave
aa ready capped fir Scotland, his faither
a sugar plantation owner, a player o sorts
but as I listen tae the kettle bile an coffee
steams the inky stains oot ma thochts

Andrew Watson's gaze turns aa sombre like
when he hears the Classifieds, his noble
Queens Park no dae'in sae well noo'adays, no
since he went sooth, gaun fae tanner ba enigma
tae bein swallied up in time added oan.

*Jim Mackintosh*

# Rèisean, Weihsian, Nollaig 1944

*Eric Liddell (1902–1945) a bhàsaich ann an campa Iapanach airson prìosanaich shìobhalta, Weihsian, Sìona.*

Tha na rèisean san robh mi
a' ruith timcheall nam cheann,
Colaiste Eltham, 100 slat, aois aon deug,
's bhuannaich mi, 's fhios a'm gun robh mi

luath. Creag Longairt, Drochaid Stamford,
Stoke-on-Trent, Paris, iad uile
a' ruith timcheall nam cheann, mo cheann
tha sgàincadh le pian. A' cuimhneachadh

nan rèisean ud, agus an rèis mhòr eile,
*chan ann do na daoine luatha an rèis ...*
*no do na daoine eòlach deagh-ghean.*
Chan eil fhios a'm am faic mi Flo

gu bràth san t-saoghal seo, m' eudail phrìseil
ann an Canada, mise nam phrìosanach cogaidh,
am faic mi gu bràth sibh? Chan eil fhios,
no am faic mi Maureen bheag a rugadh

ann an Toronto? Balla falamh air mo beulaibh
air nach fhaic mi thairis, ged bha mi luath
chan fhaigh mi thugaibh, Trish is Heather,
mo nigheanan brèagha, dìreach dealbhan dhìbh,

bloighean, smaointean, mo cheann na bhrochan,
a' cuimhneachadh gur e Gràdh an aon nì as fhiach,
a mhaireas, gèillidh mi dha, nuair a bhriseas mi
an teip, cuiridh E a làmh nam làimh,

agus bidh seo seachad.

*Maoilios Caimbeul*

# Races, Weihsian, Christmas 1944

*Eric Liddell (1902–1945) who died in a Japanese internee camp, Weihsian, China.*

The races I was in
run around in my head,
Eltham College, 100 yards, 11 years of age,
and I won, knowing well I was

fast. Craiglockhart, Stamford Bridge,
Stoke-on-Trent, Paris, they are all
running around in my head, my head
that screams with pain. Remembering

those races, and the other big race,
*the race is not to the swift…*
*or favour to the learned.*
I don't know if I'll ever

see Flo in this world, my dearest darling
is in Canada, and I a prisoner of war,
will I ever see you all? Who knows,
or will I see little Maureen born

in Toronto? A blank wall in front of me
over which I cannot see, although I was fast,
I can't get to you, Trish and Heather,
my beautiful girls, photos of you only,

fragments, thoughts, my head is mush,
remembering Love is the only worthwhile
thing that will last, I'll surrender, when I break
the tape, He will put his hand in mine,

and this will be over.

*Myles Campbell*

## BILLY BREMNER ~ ARCHIE GEMMILL

*The two footballers here represent both halves of the game; Bremner the pugnacious, combative captain of both Scotland and the Leeds United side of the 1970s matched with the artful skills of Gemmill, scorer of Scotland's most memorable World Cup goal in 1978.*

### 4

*for the sake of Leeds United*

As Joe Jordan said, Billy could make or ride the kind of tackle
that would have most players off their feet then hit
a pass as he came out of it, forty yard, precise.

When I was small, growing up two mile exactly
from where his statue stands,
the sound of a goal at Elland Road
would reach me like the bellowing of beasts.
When I heard about Minotaurs, it matched.

We were in the boys and dads enclosure
at the Gelderd End: before they built a covered stand
there was just a concrete ziggurat
that climbed into the plain white sky;
white as a Real shirt.
Bobby Collins was the captain but when the cloak fell
from the Wee Barra's shoulders that night against Torino,
Collins' thighbone broken, Billy got the job.

One Saturday, standard procedure up against
talent, some thick defender hacked him down;
they hauled him to the cinder track behind the goal;
for a moment, blood-faced and grimacing while Les Cocker
worked on him, he stared up at me,
almost close enough to touch.

He took the penalty. The net filled
like the mainsail of a fighting ship,
his leap of celebration was the bursting out
in white and bright-rust iron of exuberance itself
born from Stirling. Eddie Gray from Glasgow,
Lorimer from Dundee: theirs and Billy's flesh
and blood of Scotland set on raw Leeds grass,
them, Allan Clarke, Big Jack, Norman, battered
till we loved them more than family
as I have somehow come to love this land
that sits like rebar in the heart of life.

You can take your ginger clichés,
*he's a vicious little bastard*
*but he's our vicious little bastard*,
Dirty Leeds, all that, shove them like a boot
up Dave Mackay's broad arse.
I speak in praise of skill that football's rarely seen
and of a man who, for his adopted home,
would break himself in two.

*Harry Smart*

# Archie Gemmill Scores in a Parallel Universe

there's a loop on a screen
    in a dimly lit corner
        of the Scottish Football Museum
as if we're entering a church
    of Archie Gemmill's goal
in the 68th minute
        of the World Cup match
against Holland
    in 1978
which put Scotland 3-1 up
    for three minutes,
        and the commentator
is going ballistic
    and wee Archie
from Paisley is guiding
        the ball over Jongbloed
and punching the air
        in defiance until
the end of time


    and they've recreated
the complete ballet
    using white statues
like rejects from a Greek myth
    with the ball hanging
in mid air
    and Jongbloed
        frozen in the act of diving
    and Van der Kerkhof
looking on helplessly

and Rudi Krol
>    has the wrong number
on his shorts
with a cosmic arc of white circles
on the green carpet
>    showing the trajectory
of Archie's voyage
>    >    to immortality,
>    >    >    and Archie
>    has turned to the left
so we can all look into
>    his white bloodless face
although in reality
>    he turned to
the right

*Graham Fulton*

## BILL MCLAREN ~ ARTHUR MONTFORD

*Sports commentators are sometimes celebrated for their work behind the microphone. In Bill McLaren's case, for his humour, knowledge of the game and amiable restraint; in Arthur Montford's for flamboyant, hyperbolic outbursts laden with colourful Scots vernacular.*

## When I Hear Your Name, Bill McLaren

words come rolling into my head, words like
bracken and bonnie and blaeberry,
like kirkyard and crowdie, like moor, haar
even laverock…

words the tongue adores
for their tang of home.

I think of the fluke that tangled you up
in a sad year when I knew it was time for leaving,
was too scared-stuck to figure the way.

It's long ago and the details are dusty.
I think I was trawling for an afternoon play
to distract from my own tragi-drama,
when your voice rolled out of the radio
like something to lean on,

this mellow solid Hawick drawl, homespun
in greens and browns, sounding like something
I used to know, sounding like a man
who'd come home from his work whistling.

Everything I'd thought before about rugby
tilted. When did it get lyrical? Players playing
*like whirling tsetse flies* and *runaway bullets*,
*like demented ferrets up a wee drainpipe.*

This was commentary elevated by passion,
fired by your yearn to share; honed probably
in dedicated hours of homework.

You could easily have lured me over
to your rugged beloved sport,

if I hadn't been steeped in another *beautiful game*,
if it hadn't been the same year the clans were dream-
marching on Argentina to fetch home the World Cup.

Some year! With your memory mark on it, vivid
enduring as Archie Gemmill's redemptive goal.

The year, as it turned, when I mustered
the guts to go.  Fanciful to say
it was all down to you, but I'd swear
on a hint, a heartening, a wee knock-on
over the line.

*Maggie Rabatski*

# Arthur Montford's Horizontal Hold

...on our psyche
began with hand-held cameras
as the Hampden breeze surfed his wave of hair,
his checked sports jacket caused a stramash
with our black and white's reception
and his clipboard was all the technical backup needed.

He told us the game's excitement couldn't get any more exciting.

And he was right.
Saturday after Saturday after Saturday he was right.

Mud-glue parks, shoulder charges, goals celebrated with manly handshakes
and injuries cured by magic-sponges.

We *tumled oor wulkies* into Arthur's world.

In amongst the home grown mix of Greigs and McNeils
His measured diction tantalised us with far flung
Garrinchas, Di Stefanos, Eusebios and Yashins.

And like Tiny Wharton at an old firm match
Arthur kept us under control...

till we played in the local park
with bunched up jumpers for goalposts
and a leather bladder that could
knock you out if you headed the knotted lace.

We became Arthurs Peles and Gentos and Jinky Johnstones.

Arthur's commentary always in our heads
when we played out our ten-twenty-wanners
till the sun-set that was our final whistle each and every day.

*Brian Whittingham*

# Hooley

THE GAY GORDONS ~ THE SENSATIONAL ALEX HARVEY BAND

JIMMY SHAND ~ JACK BRUCE

EMELI SANDÉ ~ SUSAN BOYLE

THE ALEXANDER BROTHERS ~ THE PROCLAIMERS

POSTCARD RECORDS ~ CHEMIKAL UNDERGROUND

NIEL GOW ~ MARTYN BENNETT

THE BAY CITY ROLLERS ~ THE JESUS AND MARY CHAIN

THE MÒD ~ CELTIC CONNECTIONS

### THE GAY GORDONS ~ THE SENSATIONAL ALEX HARVEY BAND

*Two different ways of spending a Saturday night; the first in the company of a ceilidh band playing traditional music for dancing, the second in the rather more raucous atmosphere of a gig from one of Scotland's more notorious rock & roll bands.*

## The Gay Gordons

There's too many girls, which means they dance
        together: one leads, one follows,
but Miss still calls the moves to the men
        and the ladies from wheezing tapes,
watches, arms folded. The boys hold their partners,
        some like a pistol, some
like a turd, uncertain and furious
        at the grace of the girls with the girls.

Vince likes rugby, and Darren likes a hand
        on Vince's back in the scrum.
Darren spins Isla too loose, and Jane
        grips Vince too tight, and the boys
imagine an incomer crowd with a clutch
        of boys, quadruplets, switching
the ratio, making them dance together
        and loudly and clearly complain.

Their eyes never meet in the changing room:
        no stolen glances, no
understanding. They study each other's calves,
        peek round in the showers when
the other's not looking, in permanent terror
        of being caught. Being caught
would destroy them. And how
        would it feel to be caught, to be caught?

*Harry Giles*

# Vambo Unbound

*for Ralph MacGillivray, who was there.*

Goose-stepping onto the concert hall stage,
Long hair slicked back and parted at the side,
A cardboard moustache taped under his nose,
Alex Harvey makes the Nazi salute.

The great performer plays great dictator:
A rabble-rousing pantomime villain
Who wants his audience to boo and hiss
As he shouts *Sieg Heil!* again and again.

Shop-soiled glam rockers playing twelve-bar blues,
Punk rock apostles with nothing to lose,
Each with a weather eye on their leader,
The band keep strumming the first bars of *Framed*.

The crowd start aping Alex's actions,
As if this is a Nuremberg Rally
Being restaged in '70s Scotland
With a theme tune by Leiber and Stoller.

Harvey stops it with a chop of his hand,
Brings the music to a resounding halt;
Dropping his act, sounding broken-hearted,
He growls: *That's how it fucking well started!*

*Andrew J Wilson*

JIMMY SHAND ~ JACK BRUCE

*Think strict tempo accordion dance music and Jimmy Shand springs to mind; think electric blues/rock bass and amongst the foremost would be Jack Bruce. From* The Bluebell Polka *to* White Room *is no big step when virtuosity is taken into account.*

## Jimmy Shand

*The Albert Halls, Stirling, 1960*

Yon was music making Scottish style,
a serious business and damn hard work.
The accordion bulged like a chest expander
across the hidden muscle of his heart.
His Polkas were gales trapped in a box.
Kilted to the gills, horn specs black as coal
from the mines he went down at fourteen,
Shand gave it laldy, staring straight ahead,
unsmiling, fingers blurred, only other movement
his left heel tapping, aye on the button.
There's nothing free about expression.
He kenned that fine from earliest days.
Whatever joy there was in it for him
laboured as his father had, deep underground.

*Andrew Greig*

# Tales of Brave Ulysses

The cellist came out of the academy
to lay down his melodies
when rhythm was on the line,
only one of his crimes
delivered at a pace
on the upright bass
not all that tender
on the six string fender.

The baker walked out of the jam
till the cake was cut with Cream
congealed.
How many rope-ladders
over the bearded rainbow
would it take
to touch the moon
sure as Armstrong?
Only one –
if it was long enough
and it was.

The lyrics of fate
over four strings
sounding like eight
syncopating
the pounding heat
from the baker back on the job,
so no-one was robbed.
A guitarist just in the lead
by a narrow neck.

The three-piece
gone off the rails
but in the groove
of spinning vinyl –
Corryvreckan
in technicolour.

Shipwrecks of
wailing bluesmen.
A stumble ashore
rolling and tumbling
casting out chords
like shining barley
on a slick of honey.
A parley with the shadows
of bottle-neck heroes
and music-hall maestros.

The set of wheels
went on fire
but your covered wagon
stitched its way
across its prairie
to elegy.
A fabric
picked and unpicked
by the pricking apostrophes
of Penelope
and the tailor
you had to sing to
so his paraffin
vapourised
in the hurricane.

Many's the riff went
over the cliff.
Jack, one hell of a lad,
a banshee mourner,
tall-story teller
but a master-mariner
when all the breezes
were out
of the ministry of bag.

*Ian Stephen*

EMELI SANDÉ ~ SUSAN BOYLE

*Emeli Sandé, though Zambian by descent, grew up in Scotland, working her way up through the music scene before finding fame. West Lothian-born Susan Boyle shot to fame via* Britain's Got Talent *in 2009, going from the most unlikely of beginnings to become an overnight star.*

# Voice

It is light, and the lightness
of air, the flow of breath,
a throat full of bright vowels
that lift, and rise, and raise

in a tumble of words
rolling out on a tide
from beaches of granite,
the swell breaching rock.

It is the salt in a wound
healing as it hurts,
the sound of a woman
creating her landscape,

coursing from crag to corrie,
as water falls over stone.
Even as clouds gather,
glower, there is lightning,

skies torn apart, thundering,
there will be light, and lightness.
There are rhythms in rain, of storms,
grace in green notes, a flowering.

There is wonder, in living,
in darkness, and in the light of it,
breaking, there will be song.

*Janet Paisley*

# Susan Magdalene

I see the snarling brats
taunting you, burning
your clothes, chasing
you home from school
every miserable day.

Mine kicked wide
my toilet door, clawed
me for being clever
and, once, crushed dog-
shit into my face.

I see your bullies now
have peroxide teeth and
pound-signs in their eyes.
They pluck out your eye-
brows, fake your nails,

primp your hair and teach
you to deride yourself.
They stalk you, lapping up
footage of your anguish,
your endless fear of failing.

When I was twelve,
my bullies melted
to another school.
I heard that no good
came to them, poor kids.

I wish that I could sing
like you, into the heart
of every wounded child
before they need to hurt.
I wish that I could sing

like you, for you,
to soothe your pain
and calm your fears,
and show you that
tomorrow's looking bright.

*Valerie Thornton*

*The contrast between the two acts is clear. The Alexander Brothers, a bekilted crystallisation of Scottish clichés, and The Proclaimers – twins Craig and Charlie Reid – a jagged distillation of folk, country and soul sung in broad accents.*

## The Alexander Brothers Perform at the Dean Bowling Club, Comely Bank, Edinburgh, June 1971

I watched them from my bedroom window: two
kilted men, well-amplified (and maybe
well-oiled too), belting out their hits which flew
and heuched among the tenements. To me,
as I strained to study Tennyson, they
were pure kitsch, a local club's star turn.
*Mairi's Wedding*, then *The Bonnie River Tay*,
and how they twa had paddled in the burn.
Tom's accordion plays and the bowlers sway
then we reach the concert's climax: a wee blind lad
in an orphan's home. It could be Hogmanay!
'I'm nobody's child,' Jack croons as I go mad.
I've exams next week and I'm losing the plot.
Sing me *Mariana* or *The Lady of Shalott*.

*Jim C Wilson*

# Men

*according to The Proclaimers' songs*

A letter from America, ocean & railroad track,
a second chance, broken jaw, cigarettes
back of a bus, a slap in the puss,
cat that barks, a poor lonely heart
what it takes to be a man:
a king of the road, a drunk fighter
this man waking up next to you,
who passes every penny on to you
who would walk 1000 miles
in sorrow, sorrow.

    *Theresa Muñoz*

POSTCARD RECORDS ~ CHEMIKAL UNDERGROUND

*Two record labels; Postcard, the breezy, jangly 'Sound of Young Scotland' of the 1980s (Orange Juice, Aztec Camera), and Chemikal Underground, the dense, dark post-rock sound (Mogwai, Arab Strap) of a very different young Scotland in the 1990s.*

# Postcard

*Glasgow, February 1980*

Hi Honey,

Thanks to a horn(e) named Alan,
I'm in a shabby flat in the West End
listening to *The Sound of Young Scotland*.

Today, I heard *Orange Juice* sing. Aye,
you read right, *Orange Juice* sing.
I saw a hip-cat play a toy drum

(check the logo on the front), I
almost fell over. I hope you make it
for the birth of *Josef K*.

I'm thrilled, I love this city...
and you. X

P.S. Who needs London.

*Kevin Reid*

## A Rush A Kiss A Rush

You come to me with a white peacock
On your back with a potato with a bright star

You sing o god o delgado o merry child of Scotland
You sing because the darkness is always here

With us until the shining and then the music comes
O god o delgados o mogwai o arab strap

You come with resignation
With a rush and a kiss and a rush

You come in the night sick with drink
You come with the taste in your mouth

You sing o god o delgado o glaswegian beauty
You brush your hair from your face you sing

You sing you sing you sing you sing you sing
If only I met you when we were young

*J L Williams*

NIEL GOW ~ MARTYN BENNETT

*Two giants of traditional music: one an 18th century fiddler and composer whose songbook is still vital to musicians today; the other a Canadian-born multi-instrumentalist (1971–2005) who was at the forefront of the contemporary 'Celtic Fusion' movement.*

## Niel Gow

The blin man wuid aaweys ken yer bow sicsyne,
sic wis the fluence o yer wrist as ye played,
an fit in hobnail bit, clog, or saft calf skin
wuid step the heichtmaist fan ye reeled.

But mair important ye kent hoo tae flatter an fawn
ladies faw socht a tune by Gow named i thair honour.
Ye gar thaim wi guid braid tung an wuts weel hewn
tae kep thair place an ye yer ain, nae seekin favour.

Frae Baden Baden tae the great ha o Blair,
thay cairrit symphonies tae the gentry's parlours
an ye wuid gae thay maisters licht an air,
the tunes o Europe sailin ower heilan arbours.

Music was yer aa be it castle ha or cotter hous,
for Scottish Country Dancin echt by thirty twa
fan the Bratach Bana frae turret cairriet the news,
or kintra ceilidhs wheechin birlin, gaein thair aa.

Yer chair bides noo whaur it aaweys stuid,
waitin for the Maister's dowp tae tak its saet,
ye wir niver some mechanical fiddler cours an rude,
but a classical violin player, ane o the greats!

*George T Watt*

# Nae Regrets

*What brave new music!*
   *– Hamish Henderson, on first hearing* Grit


Bennett dead? How can he be? I'm sure
I heard him jouk & *heuch!* through birch
woods up past Hallaig just last month leading
the dead in a Seann Triubhas to Suisnish.

And not just there but in Glens Lyon & Shiel
where woodless cleared expanses reeled awake
remembering people, buildings, trees, a dance
of language dragged upright from bleeding knees.

And in Sativa, Squid, La Belle Angele,
The Buddha Bar, that's where he really is,
not dead but sampling you, me, himself
through great loops of life on a crackcorned mix.

Bennett dead? How can he be? On Mull
I saw a cliff of kilt, a ben of nodding dreads,
a bay of angry hands resolved to build
what's broken, nae words unspoken, nae regrets.


   *Stuart A Paterson*

THE BAY CITY ROLLERS ~ THE JESUS AND MARY CHAIN

*Pop sensations come and go, and Scotland has had its share over the years. The Bay City Rollers swept all before them in 1974/5 with their tartan-fringed hits. Ten years on, controversial East Kilbride band The Jesus and Mary Chain offered a darker, more visceral sound.*

## Roads Not Taken, Trousers Not Rolled

In those bye bye bygone days, we had our own echo chambers, tribes, ran in 'gangs'. Their cuffs and trouser hems jumped up to greet a redder shade of tat, while ours wore cheesecloth, maxis, too long, faded loons.

No flat whites then; we hung out in vintage style with frothy coffees at sixpence a cup on Formica tables in Janek's café where the jukebox swallowed small change and played us *Layla* and a whiter shade of pop.

It could have been so otherwise. Before the songs, the name came first in poster capitals in some forgotten holiday town. I see it still. Top of the bill: The Bay City Rollers. Who? But – cool! Except I didn't go.

Maybe the dance was cancelled. Maybe my parents said: *No*. Who knows. It might have been a summer time sensation. Just imagine if some of me had loved all of them. How close did I come to believing in their magic?

Within a year their name was everywhere. My tribe sneered and scorned to hide a shameful pride. Scottish, yes, but not ours, so no quarter given. Song leads on to prog rock concept album. I chose the less tartan way

*Eleanor Livingstone*

# The Jesus and Mary Chain

Jangling for world domination honey
(*and why do Scottish bands crave so much honey*)
you tobacco bitter sugar-mouthed boys
hard boiled lemon sweet pop
the end of the fizz
but enough for the hard candy pop
waspish for the honeysweet
buzz them in
that endless buzzing them in
that dry mouthed buzz
leave them wanting with that dry mouth buzz
iron nails down that blackbird fuzz
dry white mouths
your dry white mouths
seeking honey
singing fieldsweet summer rain & piss & honey
snagged on barbs before the world
snagged on chemical sweet barbs before the world
bottle it, boys
you got it, boys,
for all your black & white
noise, your glorious noise,
and for all that, boys,
your favourite colour
really always
was gold.

*Rachel McCrum*

# THE MÒD ~ CELTIC CONNECTIONS

*The main festival of Gaelic culture, the National Mòd features literature, song and the arts. Often referred to as the 'Whisky Olympics' but, sadly, in terms of attendance, it is small beer compared to Celtic Connections, Glasgow's annual festival of diversity and cross-fertilisation in traditional music.*

## Dùthchas Beò

*Too often parodied*
*as an over-tartaned extravaganza*
*of pitch-imperfect parrots 'still half-pissed from the night pefore'*
*the epitome of twee*
*the nadir of naff*
*the apotheosis of parochialism*
*with seditious scoring: 'Only 85 for Music? Eh? How come? Ciamar?'*

Ach an seo leam fhìn,
mìltean is bliadhnaichean air falbh
on talla luma-làn ud,
san do sheinn thusa gu dùrachdach
– sa bheil thu a' seinn an-dràsta air an rèidio –
bho bhonn cridhe a' bhoireannaich ghoirt
a b' òg a rinn a h-aomadh
*Fear an Leadain Thlàith,*
curidh tu stad orm,
bheir thu orm èisteachd
mar a thug air na h-uile a bha an làthair,
is tha do roghainn, air sgàth deagh bheusan,
gun an rann mu a leatrom a ghabhail
– measg chaileagan fo ochd bliadhn' deug –
nas truime buileach leam
air dhòigheigin a' giùlan cumhachd a' bharrachd
a-nist gur e màthair do thriùir a th' annad fhèin.

Taing dhan Àgh, smaoinichidh mi – chan e, fairichidh mi.
Taing dhan Àgh airson a' Mhòid.

*Màrtainn Mac an t-Saoir*

# Living Tradition

*Too often parodied*
*as an over-tartaned extravaganza*
*of pitch-imperfect parrots 'still half-pissed from the night pefore'*
*the epitome of twee*
*the nadir of naff*
*the apotheosis of parochialism*
*with seditious scoring: 'Only 85 for Music? Eh? How come? Ciamar?'*

But here alone in my kitchen
miles and years away
from that packed hall,
in which you sang so strongly
– in which you are now singing on the radio –
from the heart of the torn woman
who was ensnared at a young age by
*Fear an Leadain Thlàith*
*The Lad of the Lovely Hair*
you arrest me, render me able
only to stop and listen
as you did all present then,
your chaste choice to omit the verse on her pregnancy
– in an under-eighteens' competition –
all the more poignant
carrying more transformative power, now somehow
that you are a mother of three.

Thank God for the Mod, I think, no, thank God for the Mod, I feel.

*Martin MacIntyre*

# You Play the Melody

*You play the melody on the chanter*
*– Martyn Bennett,* Grit


You play the melody on the chanter
on street corners, in pubs, in concert halls,
the basements of churches and salons
in exclusive buildings, in all the forms.
Traditional is classic, and a mixing desk
brings boxes and *puirt a beul* and beats
to reels and travellers songs, and the conductor's
voice breaks as he says it. You play the melody.

We play the melody, of course we do.
We're Celts, an almost imaginary nation,
undefined in history, and known
without blood-lines or boundaries or map,
but recognised in an upbeat by the lack
of reverence for the things we cherish.
We can make them new, and keep them safe
in one burst of music. In January, in Glasgow,
anyone can be Celtic, and we're all connected.


*Elizabeth Rimmer*

# Tales

GREGORY'S GIRL ~ LOCAL HERO

BALAMORY ~ SUMMERISLE

OOR WULLIE ~ BLACK BOB

MERIDA THE BRAVE ~ MISS JEAN BRODIE

CHIC MURRAY ~ SCOTLAND THE WHAT?

BURKE & HARE ~ JEKYLL & HYDE

# GREGORY'S GIRL ~ LOCAL HERO

*A pair of contrasting movies from the hand of director Bill Forsyth, one an urban drama of teen angst, football and halting romance, the other a rural love story set against an oil boom, with the object of affection being Scotland itself.*

## Gregory's Girl

*In another million years, there'll be no men, no women. There'll just be people. Just a world full of wankers.*
     *– Eric in* Gregory's Girl

Some things are gone forever:
the clack of a typewriter under the secretary's fingers;
the gowned headmaster playing piano in the lunch hour;
the low wolf-whistles of school gardeners
greeting girls strolling past in anoraks and parkas.

*Bella bella!*

Some things are still there but transformed:
boys find *tits, bum, fanny; the lot* with one swipe on their phones;
the shops in the precincts are boarded up and forlorn
but in the homes of new towns electric toothbrushes drone
alongside laptops, iPads, Fitbits, all bought online.

*Arrivederci, Gordon.*

And other things remain the same:
for girls, being the best doesn't mean you'll make the team –
*it's not that simple* – and window cleaners still dream
of wooing bored housewives with their streak-free gleam.
Girls help each other, invisibly, behind the scenes.

          *Patricia Ace*

# Where's the Door Here?

Sky. Sea. Desire and pining. Stuff fetching
up – there is no door, only horizon.

How do you do business with a man who has
no door? Knock on the window, the long dawn.

The ethics are the same here in the north
as they are in your heart: impossible

to say... but pick up the receiver, dial;
keep watching the sky. *Sky, sir? It's amazing.*

*Jane McKie*

BALAMORY ~ SUMMERISLE

*Scotland's fictional places are often more vivid than its real ones, though Balamory, the friendly fishing village from the BBC TV children's show, is far removed from Summerisle, the island location for the cult horror movie The Wicker Man.*

## True Places

*It is not down on any map; true places never are*
  *– Herman Melville,* Moby Dick

Can you go there? Too many theres
and they don't stand still.
The pink castle's a hotel
for hunters and shooters.
The children who skipped and hopped
into the nursery
have been busy growing up,
away from Miss Hoolie.

*Can you reach it by ferry,*
*can you ride Edie's bus,*
*might you cycle with Plum*
*to the white house?*

Outside and inside don't tally:
you walk through the door
of a house in Tobermory
onto a set
somewhere in Glasgow,
all primary colours,
a red shop, a yellow turret,
a blue bus depot.

*Can you paint with Spencer,*
*play games with Josie,*
*might you meet Archie's robot*
*or buy sweets at Susie's?*

Spencer went back to Las Vegas,
of all places,
Miss Hoolie took refuge in radio
from mobs of young fans.
Plummie's at home in panto,
and Archie does stand-up,
and Susie, everyone's gran,
she died in her sleep.

*Do you still know Penny's song*
*and can you recall*
*how to make yogurt pots*
*into a castle?*

Real is not always
and worlds carve out
space on the globes
of fancy and memory.
Young folk, their thought
on exams and jobs,
could still find their way
around Balamory.

    *Sheenagh Pugh*

# Summerisle

*Dog shite and plenty af it.*
Big Tem is talking of his cucumbers,
great phalluses,
thick and rubbered enough
to crack your head.
*The carrots dinnae like it,*
*they prefer human keech.*

What luck to be born here
in this verdant space,
though our cottages slip into the sea
and we are a place
for ghosts and shotguns
and fine views of the cosmos
uncluttered by street light

because our streets are empty,
only the regeneration offices open,
winking long into the diamond night.
In Spring the auld heids
will stamp around the maypole,
their caps cocked at the breeze
and we will count the missing:

our children gone
over the hills like fairies,
their replacements grim changelings
with water for blood
the *Daily Telegraph* for a newspaper,
and not enough shite for a carrot,
if they tried all year.

*Hugh McMillan*

OOR WULLIE ~ BLACK BOB

*Think 'bucket' and to numerous Scots the image of Oor Wullie will come to mind. The popular* Sunday Post *character is, after all, 'A'body's Wullie'. If less famous, the 'Dandy Wonder Dog' Black Bob gets into – and out of – just as many scrapes.*

## Oor Wullie

Spiked hair an exclamation forest
of porcupine points and proto-punk pride,
he's unpetrified blond joie de vivre,
chutzpah charm and childhood in black
dungarees worn by not Just William.
Sitting on a philosopher's bucket
with jesters Soapy Soutar, Fat Boab and
Wee Eck, he's boy King of Auchenshoogle.

Common ownership – oors, yours, etc. –
shares the smile, that ineffable thing,
that factoid, that chiel that winna ding.
Forever in cousinhood with the Broons
in the paper only read at oor Mum's,
he declaims jings and crivens, help ma boab!
When he's the conversation, silence melts
with get-rich-quick schemes not about money.

*John Quinn*

# Black Bob (say no more)

our family dog was *dóbhran*,
a marriage of mongrels from
shetland to borders, her legs
worn down by that strange
breeding, which gave her the
ideal form for losing herself
(for days) in rabbit burrows –
she was, of course, loved,
but had those ways to upset.

what i could always predict,
was the *dandy*'s arrival, with
one dog we knew we could
trust to be attentive
to all that he was expected
to do –
this was a proxy
hound for all to whom
a dog was dream, but
we, who knew that fireside curl,
can also live in a dream,
beyond age, where andrew glen
and his faithful friend
come over the hill, come in,
and sit by our fire, to be warm

while those who shared
the name have included:
a scottish soldier, with
*a severe look and*
*a scowling eye*, hard
man, perished in battle;
a shawnee chief, one
of the last to resist
leaving indian territory;

a warhorse, son of
an irish mare, foaled at
the cape of good hope;
and there's a broad-
shouldered boxer,
ready to fight – they
offer moods. but the good
dog stays in memory,
amiable and alert, alive,

for that child's friend,
though lines on a page,
was real, was real, might
leap over the fence from his
rumpled book, and help me
round up my mother's hens,
or our neighbour's sheep –
he'd always know what to do.

*Aonghas MacNeacail*

*dóbhran: fresh-water otter (pronounced 'doh-ran')*

MERIDA THE BRAVE ~ MISS JEAN BRODIE

*Princess Merida of DunBroch, a warrior proficient with spear and sword, is the main character from the 2012 film* Brave. *In contrast, Miss Jean Brodie, a literary invention of the novelist Muriel Spark, though brave in her own way could scarcely be more refined.*

## The DunBroch Tapestry

It may have begun with the hair;
her Mother absentmindedly twirling
red shoots on her finger;
thoughts forming curls, loops,
knots, from her daughter's locks,

until something braided to her veins
made an image in the mind's loom;
laid out a familiar grid,
and her hands, quick
to pick up strands, tied it

to Merida's hair, and to a spool
where they spun onto the warp;
the rest of Merida teased,
thread by thread round the spindle
of a Mother's best intentions;

any slack tugged tight, tamped down
in the pattern, loose ends
snipped off, tucked in, so the picture
almost perfect, could be knotted.
But Merida, who would not be held,

snapped, slashed herself free
from the wool, the scrim, fled,
strings fixed in her skin
– a persistent needle.
She felt the pull.

*Keren Macpherson*

# Prime

And here entombed
is quisling Sandy,
gripping the bars,
struggling with big
questions – as if there
were questions, big
or otherwise, to be
answered or asked –
wrestling with faith,
the fragile psyche,
sin, and the world
and all its dirt.

But where's the use
in that, my dears,
my dilettanti,
when we have myth,
art and aesthetics.
Let's tramp the streets
in soft black boots,
hail and worship
gilt and glitter pagan
Caesars, find succour
in flaccid rebellions
and easy heresies.

There is no evil
where there's beauty.
That's the siren wail.
Watch the film.
Know we were born
way past our prime.

*Tim Turnbull*

## CHIC MURRAY ~ SCOTLAND THE WHAT?

*The character of a nation is often most visible through its comedy. Chic Murray offered surreal whimsy and wordplay in late-period variety theatre while the Doric-infused 'Scotland the What?' trio poked gentle fun at Scotland's way of life.*

# Chic Murray

*'What was it like? Meeting Chic
these mornings when the platform teemed
at Hillhead underground?'*

Hard now to remember. Hearing deafened by the click
and rattle of old carriages,
I could barely make out sound

or sense of any word the comic said,
*('You a wee Free that keeps the Sabbath
and anything else he gets hands on?')*

while I pondered on the motives that led
to this approach – how we both hovered over six foot?
Or if he sensed I did not belong

among these urbanites? Clan clairvoyance being exchanged?
*('I met my wife in a tunnel of love.
Each night she keeps on digging down and down.')*

Strange jests among the whispers, passing draught of subway trains
transporting souls through darkness
(like his a few months later) going deeper underground.

*Donald S Murray*

# A Day Like Today

If ever there wiz a day
A doon aboot the mooth day,
A gey dreich and drookit day
When all ye want is tae be
Beddit under the duvet

It wis the day

If ever there wiz a day
When the hale wurld seemed crazy
An affy day, when ye lost the will a wee bitty,
A day when aabudy is *thon way*
Affa shivery, a-doom's-day day

It wis the day

If ever there wiz a day
When the wurld goes frae
Bad tae wurse;
Allagrugous! Lips pursed.
Cursed! (In need o' a nurse!)

It wis the day

If ever a day, a day, a day
When ye didnae think you'd crack
A smile ne'er mind laugh till ye wur greeting, eh? (Split
Sides. Laughter's a rebellion – so it is tae.)
*Scotland the What*: the order o' the day.

It wis the day

*Jackie Kay*

BURKE & HARE ~ JEKYLL & HYDE

*One of Robert Louis Stevenson's masterpieces,* The Strange Case of Dr Jekyll and Mr Hyde, *is embedded in the gothic psyche. Equally a classic of the split personality, the infamous Burke & Hare are inextricably linked to real life 19th century horror.*

## Meeting Demand

No getting out of it now the trapdoor's
blue beneath your feet, chained to their fate
kicking at the odds.  A burking's too good for you.
The Grassmarket ghouls are harem scarem
there to see the dance between nothing
and infinity gasp again. On the slab
your belly enlightens us, the only evidence
coming kings will take from you.
Time to snap out of it.  Your once
unseen hands are tight behind your back.

The medics keep the cut they need.
Now you reap what you stitched up
out of no one missing the crop.
The only grave you ever dug was your own.
Who now shall make head nor tail
of your anatomy of greed?

*Christie Williamson*

burking, n. – *to murder, as by suffocation, so as to leave no or few marks of violence*

# The Body Snatchers

Fresh-dug earth is dug again.
In moonless dark only shrouded
lantern light. Shovels,
a crowbar, the coffin lid levered up.

A monster was rumoured, doubly nailed down
to foil defiance of death. But he lies
decent in dark broadcloth, white shirt,
the good doctor, at peace, austere.

Close by a fitful horse stamps
a hoof and shakes his harnessed head.
They reach to raise the pale cadaver
from a solitary, unforgiving bed.

The doctor, whose uncallused fingers touched
the untouched flesh of young girls.
They reach, but then recoil in horror.
The coarse black hair on the doctor's knuckles,

a subtle metamorphosis of features.
The body thickens. The lantern falls
with a dull rattle. But reward beckons,
science and the anatomist await,

keen to know if under the skin
there is blood and bone like any other.
They falter as they lift and wrap rough sacks
around their burden. The horse trots

through the black night. They take the money,
down a dram to calm their shaking hands.
At home their wives and children sleep.
The sun will rise. The anatomist will bid

his students to take careful note
as he makes the first cut. They must not
close their eyes. Heart, lungs, muscle,
the brain's excesses. It's dangerous to dream.

He smiles. *You may think*, he says,
*the dead are silent. You would be wrong.*
*The hollow skull can talk. The liver*
*and the lights have tales to tell.*

He tilts his head, studies the smooth
and naked limbs, seeks in vain a hint
of hidden ruin, the signature of Satan
on the untroubled face. The scalpel cuts.

Their children play. Their wives
don't ask how food is put upon
the table. Not one but truly two.
Every human soul is double.

A headstone at the empty grave.
*Dr Henry Jekyll, admired physician,*
*benefactor, upright citizen.*
The heart revealed, can science
truly know if the man who died
was Dr Jekyll or Mr Hyde?

*Jenni Daiches*

# Notions

THE COLOURISTS ~ THE GLASGOW BOYS

ALEXANDER GRAHAM BELL ~ JOHN LOGIE BAIRD

WEALTH OF NATIONS ~ LOGARITHMS

LORD KELVIN ~ SIR PETER HIGGS

BURNS NIGHT ~ UP-HELLY-AA

ROBERT ADAM ~ KEIR HARDIE

NORTH BRITAIN ~ CALEDONIA

THE COLOURISTS ~ THE GLASGOW BOYS

*Active in the late Victorian period, the Glasgow Boys were practitioners of an innovatory impressionism in Scottish painting. In the first decades of last century the Scottish Colourists were remarkable for their vibrant waves of colour in both interiors and landscapes.*

## Cadell (and other Colourists)

*Live like a bourgeois, work like a demi-God.*
   *– Flaubert*


He was a man who'd looked long at the sea
And islandscaped his visions of Iona.
His other habitat was Edinburgh rooms –
George Street, Ainslie Place, Regency Terrace –
And their vocabulary of furniture,
Crockery, silverware, mirrors, polished floors,
Prosperous Georgian interiors.
And fashionable women, seldom smiling –
Thirty-something? Forty-something? Hard to tell,
In their melodic black millinery.
Age, anyway, as geniuses portray it,
Becomes timeless, although in its moment.
But, best of all, it's colours that say it –
*The Black Hat* – there's several of these – *The White Room*,
*The Red Chair, The Orange Blind, The Tapestry Cloak.*
So much leisure… But I feel something tense,
Or sorrowful, in all that elegance.
Who were the dress-makers and milliners?
Who made the mirrors shine, who cleaned the grate,
Who set the table that fine afternoon?
Could it be imagined and fictitious,
Reality transformed by liliaceous
Peploe, Cadell, and muscular Fergusson.


   *Douglas Dunn*

# In a Good Light

Guthrie came here first. It's for the light,
he said. Light's everywhere, I know,
but all along this coast it feels like
there's more of it to go round.

There's short winter light, cloud-softened,
diffuse, but still strong enough for detail
and colour. Summer light sparkles
on the sea, shimmers in the trees.

Walton, Henry, Crawhall and the rest –
'The Boys' – came and left,
but Guthrie stayed, light-borne,
seasonally sombre, seasonably bright.

They sketched in the village and the fields,
transforming cobbles, pantiles, the faces
of children and old men, from French Realism
to something native, local, universal.

I look at a cabbage-patch girl, knife in hand,
face tanned by Merse sun, her cool stare,
about to sned one for the pot, tonight's supper.
They grow well here, kail and daughters.

Something in the light makes them strong,
sonsy, striking subjects for portraits.
This is how we are, she says, this is how
I am, en plein air, standing in the light.

*Colin Will*

ALEXANDER GRAHAM BELL ~ JOHN LOGIE BAIRD

*Scottish ingenuity has often transformed the world. Edinburgh native Alexander Graham Bell patented the first telephone in 1876 while Helensburgh-born inventor John Logie Baird gave us the first television pictures in 1925.*

# Memoir Concerning the Transmission of Speech

You did not consider yourself an inventor
though you tuned the telegraph's electric codes
to clone voices from the shapes of waves

a machine for the transmission of speech
it made you one of the speculative elect.

You did not consider yourself an inventor
you taught the deaf to decipher meaning
to articulate words through visible speech

a child's hands tied behind her back
not violence   a necessity of assimilation.

You did not consider yourself an inventor
of cruelties   or divisions   or constructs
your speculative mind simply invented devices

to locate icebergs   split salt from seawater
the photophone   a posting of speech by sunlight
a conversation clouded by weather

as the transmission of sound was clouded
by your notions of hereditary deafness
of a nation diminished by defective genes.

You did not consider yourself an inventor
but a thinker concerned to prevent
*a deaf variety of the human race*

love and its transmission
by a visible speech you reckoned primitive
foreign   as weakness or difference

the gestures   the facial grimace of signs
its visual alphabet and spatial grammar
the hand and the face making a poem of the deaf

a commonality and communication
that were not yours

to which you were not listening.

*Gerrie Fellows*

## Stooky Bill

An old tea chest,
biscuit tin, hat box,
scissors, darning needles,
glue and sealing wax,
were among the ingredients
John Logie Baird chose to mix
into his 'machine for seeing
by wireless.'

Some thought he was a lunatic.
One feared he might have a razor.
All he had was a 'televisor'
and Stooky Bill,
a ventriloquist dummy
who'd turn out to be
the first face transmitted
via primitive television.

Imagine his first demonstration,
Stooky Bill under arm,
he tries to explain his machine
like a performer everyone laughs at
on a talent show broadcast
into millions of living rooms
a century after
the dummy's performance.

*Ross Wilson*

WEALTH OF NATIONS ~ LOGARITHMS

*John Napier's 17th century discovery of logarithms paved the way for modern mathematics and ultimately for the development of the computer. The following century Adam Smith laid the foundations for economic capitalism with his book* The Wealth of Nations.

# A Twenty Pound Note

*Ultimately, [Adam Smith realised] wealth is not money – it is the amount of other people's labour that we can command, or purchase.*
  *– Eamonn Butler,* The Condensed Wealth of Nations

So how am I to think of this red note –
the rough equivalent of a chef bought for
two hours – without the food or steaming kitchen –
just the clean movement of profession: cutting,
filleting, seasoning the air with air,
since nothing else, then bringing it to me;

or send him away, and make it forty minutes
of a tailor – with him pinning his pale samples
of daylight to my waist, chalking lines, without
the chalk, when measuring me – or send him away,
and make it just a lawyer for ten minutes,
pulling an absent book from an absent shelf,

then calling time; just don't make it a planter
from a coffee farm, or fruit grove harvester:
gathering, yes – and sowing, yes – and lifting
their body on, all muscle and thumbed rib,
but for days and days and days – for me;
then, what, I tender this into their hand?

  *Niall Campbell*

# Great Powers: John Napier of Merchiston

Nautilus shell spirals outwards,
sunflower seed-head spirals in;
nature's patterning.

*Marvellous Merchiston* the man,
after twenty years making his tables,
ten million numbers long,
breaks the heavens wide
open, shortens their labour to
double astronomers' lives.

The hawk spiralling to its prey
a hurricane's brutal arms;
nature's patterning.

Raising numbers to powers
for huge steps across
the solar system,
binding planets to sun.
Adding, subtracting powers,
taming numbers whose
magnitude in multiplication
mashes brains
into boggled jelly.

The nerves of the cornea,
a Catherine wheel spiral;
nature's patterning.

Four days London to Edinburgh,
soil baked, horses panting
in the summer drought;
then they gaze, silent, for long minutes:
Briggs, Napier; Napier, Briggs;
*your engine of wit or ingenuity.*
Two years until Napier lays
his real bones down for good.

And so we master the false
infinity of grains of sand:
two numbers net up every molecule
from this beach to furthest galaxies:
*ten times* itself,
*eighty* times.

*Ruth Aylett*

LORD KELVIN ~ SIR PETER HIGGS

*Scotland does science very well. At Edinburgh University Peter Higgs probed the nature of the universe through his discovery of the Higgs Boson particle. Victorian physicist Lord Kelvin made great discoveries in thermodynamics and engineering.*

# Happens

*The Higgs Boson is estimated... to travel less than a billionth of an inch between when it's produced and when it decays.*
— Sean Carroll, The Particle at the End of the Universe

*Grandparents' voices uninterruptedly talking, in Eternity.*
— Elizabeth Bishop, The Moose

things happen

a bus moves slowly on a forest road
some thin mist, night coming on
the passengers talk about grandchildren
and weather and who's died
and who's still with us by the grace of God

a woman leans her head against the window
a moose steps from the trees

or in the Large Hadron Collider at CERN
in proton collisions glowing on a screen
the merest hint of the merest shiver
of everything there is

for a moment, the world looks back at us
fathomable, real

the trembling of a particle
a moose, moonlit and still, at the edge of a wood –
things happen and are held
and are gone

everything is touch and go
communion and decay

and we're left with  – what exactly?

*in a white vase on a mahogany table*
*the tulips are beginning to die*

*rainy April light fills the dining room window*

*somewhere a bird long asleep*
*sings its blue awakening*

*Chris Powici*

# One Proof for Lord Kelvin's Second Law of Thermodynamics

Heat will not flow from a colder body to a hotter body
Heat will not flow from an older body to a hotter toddy
Heat will not flow from a gaudy folder to a shoddy jotter
Heat will not flow from a modern moulder to an orthodox potter
Heat will not flow from a smallish smoulder to a Guy Fawkes plotter
Heat will not flow from a proud householder to a soapbox squatter
Heat will not flow from a rich shareholder to a foreign slaughter
Heat will not flow from your cold shoulder
Heat will not flow from you
Heat will not know you
Heat will not glow
Heat will slow
Heat will go
Heat will
Go cold
In you

*Jim Carruth*

BURNS NIGHT ~ UP-HELLY-AA

*Falling at the end of January these two celebrations are very different events. One is a commemoration of lyric poetry and social commentary while the other is a Norse festival of drama and fire, so far-removed from Burns's Scotland as to seem almost another country.*

## Grace

Some have meat
and some have friends to gather

close some nights, hot
in those cold places so often

between us – my how you whistle & slope
and make welcome in our gory bed

while the plough drones sleek
and bomb the land with barrels

so what, we tae a moose,
we wee timorous beasties

so what, I am sorry, night
and I am sorry Burns

that we've not done more
with that space between us

we sing with the wind
at our backs, and growl

when rain has teeth
the price of meat

keeps rising – like blood
to stiffen our resolve

to thank
for what we have.

*Ryan Van Winkle*

# Hamefarin

*Up-Helly-Aa, 2012*

Da live webcast plays
on da lowest bandwidth
until da piktur
freezes

an I'm left stoorin
hit clesters o azin pixels
lik lowsin burns
wenglin intae a skrotti voe
i da hert-holl o da screen.

I wait a start.
Somewhaar i da tenement
kums da hushie-baa
o a cistern. Sirens gowl
ootside. A fozie mön
glinders ower da city's
scordet skin.

Da peerie buffer wheel
keeps spinnin.

Da mirknin sinks
hits yackels i da room.
I dis dim, da screen faas a hert-stane,
a cassen glöd.

*Roseanne Watt*

# Homecoming
*Up-Helly-Aa, 2012*

The live webcast plays
on the lowest bandwidth
until the picture
freezes

and I'm left staring
at messes of blazing pixels
like bright burns
twisting and turning into a red-orange sea-loch
in the middle of the screen.

I wait a moment.
Somewhere in the tenement
comes the lullaby
of a cistern. Sirens howl
outside. A soft and sapless moon
peers through half-shut eyes over the city's
cracked skin.

The little buffer wheel
keeps spinning.

The darkness sinks
its teeth into the room.
In this dusk, the screen becomes a hearth,
a sullied, decaying glow.

      *Roseanne Watt*

## ROBERT ADAM ~ KEIR HARDIE

*Both dedicated to changing the world, though in very different ways, architect Robert Adam was a leader of the classical revival in the late 1700s, while Keir Hardie, a founder of the Labour Party, became the first Labour MP at Westminster in 1892.*

## Bob the Roman

We can't see Rome every day
and the thought of mis-spending so much time
among a most ridiculous set
of gamesters to no purpose –

I seek an unconstrained and noble way
of thinking and talking
and have resolved to lay aside
the fike-faks of company.

The town rich with domes, spires
and lofty buildings I walk much about
and sketch after the antiques;
I feast on marble ladies,

dance attendance in
the chamber of Venus, trip
a minuet with old Otho
and all those other Roman worthies.

Thus metamorphosed
learning to draw ruins to perfection
living unmolested by kirk or state
I am here like the King of Artists.

*Ken Cockburn*

Robert Adam (1728–92) spent just over two years in Rome, from February 1755 to May 1757. The text of the poem is adapted from his letters written at that time.

# James Keir Hardie

Tae Friedrich Engels ye were the *super cunning Scot… with demagogic tricks*
an he wisnae sookin in. Hud he been a kirkie mannie,
he'd huv been doon oan his knees, pittin up a wird
makin siccar ye niver got nar sniffin distance o Westminster.
His girnin wraxed new heichts faan ye waaked throu that door,
claith bunnet an hamespun, spleet-new Member for West Ham.

Nae for you the cauld analysis, the lang-nebbit theory o the dialectic
settin the warld tae richts. Aa yer gumption, yer scrievin, yer wirds
cam fae life, fae a day's lang darg, fae the hard tyauve o yer hauns
burnt intae muscle memory – aa these oors sittin in the derkness
ten year auld, listenin for the rummle o each loaded cairt
managin tae practise yer letters gin ye'd a caunle stump.

Men voted for ye ower the heids o the weel-gaithert, the swall-heidit,
the high-bendit. An it wisnae jist cause o yer kittlin-up wirds,
though you cud start a bleeze in ony owdience – aye, an relish it!
Workin fowk were gizzent in weys the theorists hud nae idea.
But you did – an mair. Ilka chiel that voted for ye kent yer years in the pit,
pyochered the coal blaik in yer lungs, daured the beat o yer contermit hert.

Nae that ye were athoot principle. Ye were niver a pragmatist. An wirds
were yer freens. A scriever in papers, leaflets, aftentimes awa fae hame
warld traiveller, warly-wise – yet ye keepit yer watch at Cumnock time
*for I could tell then, what was going on at home…*
*when the children went to school, when they returned*
*when they went to bed…*

For that alane, I'd huv voted for ye.

*Sheila Templeton*

*Whatever the truth of what Scotland truly is – or was – lies somewhere between the terms 'North Britain' and 'Caledonia', the former dating from the 18th century but now abandoned, the latter still current, though originating in the distant past.*

## North Britain

*On examining the provenance of a carte-de-visite by the 19th century St Andrews photographer Thomas Roger.*

This carte-de-visite is a note
a caller left at our door, in a past
as familiar to us as its own invention:
the sepia tones that it's taught us
were ever the favoured garb;

one we expect like watch chains
and fobs, bustles and Paisley shawls,
a neck brace hidden between the folds.
But text embossed upon the reverse
offers a moment of pause

image and pose don't contain:
fashion intent on hiding what's been
cast aside, so passé that Scotland needs
must be concealed, hidden behind
its absence. N B here noted well.

*Brian Johnstone*

# Caledonia

*Caldonia! Caldonia!*
*What makes your big head so hard?*
    Louis Jordan and the Tympany Five


I don't know if you can see
my name on the label mum had sewn
into my shirts. It's there for me,
my friend, so when I am alone

I can take a keek under my collar,
mind the man I used to be before
I pitched up in these parts, smaller,
dumber than the sum of the wars

we fought with you. Back then I
was lean and lanky, great big feet,
ignorant of how the land and sky
could be unfolded like a sheet

before me and beyond, waking
sooner every day to forest choirs
and corbie calls, the shaking
of the land by sea, persistent fires

long put out in places I had drifted
from. Mama said *son, keep away*
*from there, its grudges and its frigid*
*people, lousy with laments, the day*

*long gone when anyone might ask*
*them what they know or think*
but all she saw were English masks,
the jokes recalled in midst of drink,

the history that wasn't hers. I've been
telling new stories, singing songs
I do not own, watching submarines
put out to sea, their payloads long

unwanted. I see how the nation breaks
and blends and bonds. I'm scarred
for life, but maybe that is what it takes,
what it is that makes our big heads hard.

*Andy Jackson*

# Biographies

PATRICIA ACE has published *First Blood* (HappenStance, 2006) and *Fabulous Beast* (Freight Books, 2013). Her work appears in *Be the First to Like This: New Scottish Poetry* (Vagabond Voices, 2014), *Hallelujah For 50ft Women: Poems about Women's Relationship to their Bodies* (Bloodaxe, 2015) and *Umbrellas of Edinburgh* (Freight Books, 2016).

KATE ARMSTRONG has taught Scots language in schools and Creative Writing in Dundee, and worked with poetry translation classes in Liège. She has produced one collection. Her work has been published in a number of anthologies, the latest *A Kist o Skinklan Things* (ASLS 2016). She lives in Dundee.

CLAIRE ASKEW's poetry collection *This changes things* (Bloodaxe, 2016), was shortlisted for the Edwin Morgan Poetry Award and the Saltire First Book Prize. Her debut novel, *All The Hidden Truths* (Hodder, 2018), won the 2016 Lucy Cavendish Fiction Prize and was a *Times* Crime Book of the Month. She is Writer in Residence at the University of Edinburgh.

JEAN ATKIN's family came from Shetland and for years she lived in Dumfries & Galloway. Her new collection *How Time is in Fields* is forthcoming from IDP in 2019, and her previous collection *Not Lost Since Last Time* is published by Oversteps Books. Recent work has appeared in magazines including *The Rialto*, *Agenda*, *Ambit* and *Magma*, and commissioned by Radio 4. www.jeanatkin.com

JANETTE AYACHI is a Scottish-Algerian poet published in over 70 literary journals/anthologies. She is the author of *Pauses at Zebra Crossings* and *A Choir of Ghosts*. Her first full collection *Hand Over Mouth Music* will be published by Pavilion (University of Liverpool, 2019). She is currently working on *Lonerlust*, a nonfiction narrative about travelling alone.

RUTH AYLETT lives in Edinburgh and teaches and researches university-level computing. She jointly authored the pamphlet *Handfast* in 2016 and performed with Sarah the Poetic Robot at the 2012 Edinburgh Free Fringe. Published by *Antiphon*, *Prole*, *Envoi*, Bloodaxe Books, *Poetry Scotland*, Red Squirrel Press and others. www.macs.hw.ac.uk/~ruth/writing.html.

FRAN BAILLIE has been published in *Gutter, Lunar, Sentinel, FWS, Southlight, Poet's Republic, Prole* and others. Commended in the William Soutar Writing Prize and shortlisted in The Plough Prize, she has recently had a poem and a pamphlet, *Mixter-Maxter*, published by Grey Hen and is compiling a collection about Catholicism and about her mother.

COLIN BEGG is a writer, editor and doctor from Ayrshire. He is co-editor/co-founder of *Gutter* magazine. His poems have appeared in periodicals from *Poetry Scotland* to *The British Journal of Psychiatry*, and in *New Writ-*

*ing Scotland*. He is a recipient of a Hawthornden Fellowship and a winner of the Basil Bunting Poetry Award, and is currently working on his first poetry collection.

TESSA BERRING is an Edinburgh based artist and writer. Her most recent work appears in *The Rialto*, *Zarf Poetry* (in collaboration with Kathrine Sowerby), and *Rabbit Catastrophe Review*. Her sequence of short poems, *Cut Glass and No Flowers* was published by Dancing Girl Press in June 2017.

SHEENA BLACKHALL is a poet, writer and traditional ballad singer from the North East of Scotland. She has published four Scots novellas, ten short story collections and well over 100 poetry collections. Recently she translated *Of Mice and Men*, *The Winnerfu Warlock o Oz*, and *Dr Jekyll & Mr Hyde* into Doric. She has also published books for children.

MAOILIOS CAIMBEUL/MYLES CAMPBELL was born in 1944 in the Isle of Skye. He writes mainly in Gaelic and has published six poetry collections, plus two co-authored volumes. He has written eight novels for youngsters. His latest work is a verse dialogue *An Dà Anam/In Two Minds* with Diarmuid Johnson.

ANGUS PETER CAMPBELL/AONGHAS PÀDRAIG CAIMBEUL is a poet, novelist and actor. He was born and brought up in South Uist and went to Oban High School where his English teacher was Iain Crichton Smith. His novel *Memory and Straw* (Luath Press) won the Saltire Fiction Award, 2017. His most recent work is the bilingual (Gaelic/English) poetry collection *Stèisean* (Luath, 2018).

CATRIONA LEXY CAMPBELL is a theatre artist and writer; publishing poetry, novels, scripts and childrens' books. She was Writer in Residence at Sabhal Mòr Ostaig in 2013. She is Creative Learning Manager with Theatre Gu Leòr and has toured two plays with the company, *Doras Dùinte* (2014) and *Shrapnel* (2016).

NIALL CAMPBELL is from the Western Isles. His first collection *Moontide*, winner of the Saltire First Book of the Year and the Edwin Morgan Poetry Award, was published by Bloodaxe in 2014. *First Nights*, poems from *Moontide* plus new work, appeared in the US in the Princeton Series of Contemporary Poets in 2016.

JIM CARRUTH is the current Glasgow Poet Laureate. He is co-founder of St Mungo's Mirrorball and artistic adviser of StAnza. His first book *Killochries*, was shortlisted for the Fenton Aldeburgh award and the Saltire Scottish Poetry Book of the Year in 2015. His second *Black Cart* came out in 2017.

A C CLARKE lives in Glasgow and is a member of Scottish PEN. Her fourth collection, *In The Margin* (Cinnamon Press), appeared in 2015. *Owersettin*, her pamphlet in collaboration with Sheila Templeton and Maggie Rabatski, was published by Tapsalteerie in 2017. *A Troubling Woman* was published in 2017 and her prizewinning pamphlet *War Baby* in 2018.

KEN COCKBURN is a freelance poet and translator based in Edinburgh, where he also runs Edinburgh Poetry Tours. Recent publications include *Floating the Woods*; *Gleann Badraig*, with photographer Charles March; and *Heroines from Abroad*, translations of poems by Christine Marendon (all 2018). www.kencockburn.co.uk

STEWART CONN is a poet and playwright. His publications include *The Breakfast Room* (2011 Scottish Poetry Book of the Year) and *The Touch of Time: New & Selected Poems* (Bloodaxe) and most recently *Against the Light* (Mariscat). Edinburgh's inaugural Makar from 2002–2005, he reads his work on The Poetry Archive.

ROBERT CRAWFORD's first collection of poems was *A Scottish Assembly* (Chatto, 1990); his most recent collections are *The Scottish Ambassador* (Cape, 2018) and the Scots poetry book *Chinese Makars* (Easel Press, 2016). He is Professor of Modern Scottish Literature at the University of St Andrews, and editor of *The Book of Iona* (Polygon, 2016).

IAN CROCKATT is a prize-winning poet and poetry translator. He has published ten collections of poetry and poetry translations in book, chapbook, e-book and CD forms. His latest book is *The Song Weigher: Complete Poems of Egill Skallagrímsson, Tenth Century Viking and Skald* (Arc Publications, 2017).

JENNI DAICHES lives in South Queensferry. Published poetry includes *Mediterranean* (1995) and *Smoke* (2005). She writes on literary and historical subjects as Jenni Calder. Fiction includes *Letters from the Great Wall* (2006), *Forgive* (2015) and *Borrowed Time* (2016). Recent non-fiction includes *Essence of Edinburgh: An Eccentric Odyssey* (2018).

CLAUDIA DAVENTRY moved to St Andrews, often said not to be wholly Scottish, from Amsterdam, maintaining the itinerant lifestyle of her family, who were also not wholly Scottish. Her work has won several awards, including the Bridport and the inaugural Ruskin prizes and a Templar award in 2015 for her pamphlet *The Oligarch Loses His Patience*.

CHRISTINE DE LUCA, who writes in both English and Shetlandic, served as Edinburgh's Makar from 2014 to 2017. Her latest collection, *Dat Trickster Sun* (Mariscat, 2014) was shortlisted for the Michael Marks Poetry Pamphlet Prize. Her poems have been selected four times for the Best Scottish Poems of the Year.

IMTIAZ DHARKER is a poet, artist and documentary film-maker. Awarded the Queen's Gold Medal for Poetry in 2014, she is a recipient of the Cholmondeley

Award and a Fellow of the Royal Society of Literature. Her sixth collection of poems, *Luck is the Hook*, was published by Bloodaxe Books, 2018.

DOUGLAS DUNN is a poet, short-story writer, critic and editor. His most recent collection is *The Noise of a Fly* (Faber, 2017). He received the OBE in 2003, and the Queen's Gold Medal for Poetry in 2013. He was Professor of English at the University of St Andrews 1991–2008.

VICKI FEAVER moved to Dunsyre, South Lanarkshire in 2000. Her collection, *The Handless Maiden* (Cape 1994), gained a Heinemann Award and was shortlisted for the Costa Prize. *The Book of Blood* (Cape 2006) was shortlisted for the Costa and Forward Prizes. 'Judith' won the Forward Prize for Best Single Poem in 1993.

GERRIE FELLOWS' fifth collection, *Uncommon Place*, is forthcoming from Shearsman in 2019. Her work includes *The Body in Space* and several sequences exploring the effects of technologies on places and people: hydro-electricity in *The Powerlines* and in-vitro fertilisation in *Window for a Small Blue Child*.

MATTHEW FITT is a makar and translator. Author o *But n Ben A-Go-Go*, the first science-fiction novel in Scots, he is co-foonder o Itchy Coo. A Scots columnist for *The National* newspaper, he is the official Scots translator o *Harry Potter and the Philosopher's Stane*. *www.mfitt.com*

GRAHAM FULTON has had 15 full-length collections published including *Equal Night* (Salmon Poetry, 2017), *Paragraphs at the End of the World* (Penniless Press, 2016), *Brian Wilson in Swansea Bus Station* (Red Squirrel Press, 2015) and *Open Plan* (Smokestack Books, 2011). *Flesh and Stone* was published in 2018.

MAGI GIBSON's collections include *Graffiti in Red Lipstick*, *Wild Women of a Certain Age* and *Washing Hugh MacDiarmid's Socks* (Luath, 2017). Poems are in *Modern Scottish Women Poets* (Canongate), *Scottish Love Poems* (Canongate), *The Edinburgh Book of Twentieth Century Scottish Poetry* (EUP). *The Senile Dimension* won the Scotland on Sunday/Women 2000 Writing Prize.

HARRY GILES is from Orkney and lives in Edinburgh. Their latest collection is *The Games* from Outspoken Press, shortlisted for the Edwin Morgan Poetry Award. They were the 2009 BBC Scotland slam champion, they co-direct the live art platform ANATOMY, and have toured participatory theatre across Europe and Leith. *www.harrygiles.org*

MARJORIE LOTFI GILL was the first Poet in Residence at Jupiter Artland, Spring Fling and the 2015 Wigtown Book Festival. Marjorie's poems have been widely published in the UK and USA (including in *The Scotsman, Gutter, Magma, Rattle* and *The Rialto*) and have been performed on BBC Radio 4. Her pamphlet *Refuge* is published by Tapsalteerie Press.

JOHN GLENDAY is the author of four collections of poetry. *The Apple Ghost* received a Scottish Arts Council Book Award; *Grain* was shortlisted for both the Ted Hughes Award and the Griffin International Poetry Prize. His most recent *The Golden Mean* won the 2015 Roehampton Poetry Prize.

RODY GORMAN was born in Dublin in 1960 and lives in Skye. He has published a dozen collections of poetry. *Chernilo*, his selected poems in Irish and Scottish Gaelic, was published by Coiscéim in 2006.

STEPHANIE GREEN's pamphlet *Flout* was published by HappenStance, 2015. Her poetry has been set to music by Marisa Sharon Hartanto at the St Magnus Festival, 2013, and has also inspired a dance choreographed by Matthew Hawkins, Edinburgh, 2015. *Berlin Umbrella,* a collaboration with Sound Artiste Sonja Heyer, launched in Berlin in June 2018. She is also a dance and theatre reviewer. *https://sites.google.com/site/stephgreen1/*

AIKO GREIG, born in California, lives in Scotland where she completed an MSc in Creative Writing at the University of Edinburgh. Aiko won a Scottish Book Trust New Writers Award in 2015. Her poetry is published in *The Edinburgh Review*, *Dactyl*, and *Ink Sweat & Tears*, among others. *www.lionandsloth.com*

ANDREW GREIG, born in Bannockburn, lives in Edinburgh and Orkney with wife, novelist Lesley Glaister. A full-time writer and part-time banjoist, he has written over 20 books of poetry, novels and non-fiction, most recently *You Know What You Could Be* (with Mike Heron). He recommends Richard Thompson's classic 'Don't Sit On My Jimmy Shands'. *www.andrew-greig.weebly.com*

MANDY HAGGITH is a writer and forest activist based in Assynt. Her poetry collections include *letting light in, Castings* and *A-B-Tree*. She edited the tree poetry anthology *Into the Forest*. She also writes novels, non-fiction and plays, and her latest novel, *The Walrus Mutterer*, is a Historical Novels Society editor's choice. *www.mandyhaggith.net*

W N HERBERT is mostly published by Bloodaxe Books. Recent volumes include *Omnesia* and, with Donut Press, *Murder Bear* (both 2013). He is Professor of Poetry and Creative Writing at Newcastle University, and Dundee's Makar/City Laureate. In 2014 he won a Cholmondeley Award, and in 2015 was made a Fellow of the Royal Literary Society.

TRACEY HERD lives in Dundee. She was Creative Writing Fellow at Dundee University (1998–2001). She has published three collections with Bloodaxe: *No Hiding Place* (1996), shortlisted for the Forward Prize for Best First Collection; *Dead Redhead* (2001), Poetry Book Society Recommendation; and *Not in This World* (2015), shortlisted for the T S Eliot Prize.

RUSSELL JONES is an Edinburgh-based writer and editor. He has published five poetry collections and edited three poetry anthologies. He is deputy editor of *Shoreline of Infinity*, a sci-fi magazine, writes SFF fiction and is the UK Pet Poet Laureate. *WriterRussellJones.blogspot.com*

JACKIE KAY was born and brought up in Scotland. She has published five collections of poetry for adults – *The Adoption Papers,* awarded the Forward Prize, a Saltire Award and an SAC Book Award – and several for children. She was awarded an MBE in 2006. In March 2016, she was appointed the Makar/National Poet of Scotland.

DAVID KINLOCH has published five collections of poetry, the last three with Carcanet Press. His latest book, *In Search of Dustie-Fute*, was published by Carcanet in 2017 and was shortlisted for a Saltire Award. He is currently Professor of Poetry and Creative Writing at the University of Strathclyde.

PIPPA LITTLE is a Scots poet living in Northumberland. Her second collection is *Twist* (Arc, 2017); her first, *Overwintering*, was shortlisted for The Seamus Heaney Centre Prize in 2012. Her poems appear in *The Rialto, TLS, New Statesman* and *Poetry Review* and in many anthologies. Her first job was with D C Thomson on *The People's Friend.*

ELEANOR LIVINGSTONE lives in Fife. Her first full collection, *Even the Sea* (Red Squirrel Press, 2010), now in a second edition, was shortlisted for the 2010 inaugural London New Poetry award for first collections. She is the Director of StAnza, Scotland's International Poetry Festival which takes place annually. *www.stanzapoetry.org.*

GERRY LOOSE is a poet and artist working primarily with the natural world as well as the world of geo-politics. His work is found inscribed and created in parks, botanic gardens and natural landscapes, also in galleries and on the page. His most recent publications are *Night Exposures* and *Fault Line* (both Vagabond Voices) and *An Oakwoods Almanac* (Shearsman Books).

MÀRTAINN MAC AN T-SAOIR/MARTIN MACINTYRE is an author, poet and storyteller. His latest short story collection, *Cala Bendita's a Bheannachdan* (2014) was shortlisted for The Saltire Literary Book of the Year. His early poetry was published bilingually in *Dannsam Led Fhaileas/Let Me Dance With Your Shadow*. In 2007, he was crowned 'Bàrd' by An Comunn Gàidhealach.

LINDSAY MACGREGOR co-hosts *Platform*, the regular poetry and music night, at Ladybank Station in Fife. Her debut pamphlet, *The Weepers*, is published by Calder Wood Press. In 2015, she received a Scottish Book Trust New Writer's Award.

ROB A MACKENZIE was born in Glasgow and lives in Leith. He has published two pamphlets and two full poetry collections, the most recent being *The*

*Good News* (Salt, 2013). His poems, reviews and articles have appeared in various publications. He is reviews editor of *Magma Poetry* magazine.

JIM MACKINTOSH is a Perth-based poet. He is author of six collections, most recently *Flipstones* (Tippermuir Books, 2018). He is editor of *Mind the Time* (2017), an anthology of poetry for the Football Memories project which supports the work of Alzheimer Scotland. He is Poet-in-Residence for St Johnstone FC.

AONGHAS MACNEACAIL, trilingual poet, songwriter, journalist, holds many literary awards. ASLS Fellowship, D.Litt from Glasgow University. Collections: *An Seachnadh (The Avoiding), Oideachadh Ceart (A Proper Schooling), Laoidh an Donais Oig (Hymn to a Young Demon), Rock and Water*, and in Scots, *Ayont the Dyke*. His new and selected is *Deanamh Gàire ris a Chleoc (Laughing at the Clock)*. www.aonghasmacneacail.co.uk

KEREN MACPHERSON trained as a painter in Edinburgh. She completed her MLitt at Dundee University in 2015. She lived in New Jersey and Colorado for fifteen years working as an artist and an art teacher. She has had poems published in *New Writing Dundee, Dundee Writes*, and *Seagate III*.

RICHIE MCCAFFERY is the author of the collections *Passport* and *Cairn* from Nine Arches Press. He was the editor of *Finishing the Picture: The Collected Poems of Ian Abbot*. An academic edited collection on the work of Sydney Goodsir Smith is forthcoming with Brill.

MARION MCCREADY lives in Dunoon, Argyll. She is a winner of the Scottish Book Trust New Writers Award and also the Melita Hume Poetry Prize. Her first full-length collection, *Tree Language*, was published by Eyewear Publishing (2014). Her second collection, *Madame Ecosse*, was also published by Eyewear Publishing (2017).

RACHEL MCCRUM won the 2012 Callum MacDonald Award for her first pamphlet *The Glassblower Dances*; was inaugural BBC Scotland Poet In Residence in 2015 and received a Robert Louis Stevenson Fellowship in 2016. Her first full collection *The First Blast To Awaken Women Degenerate* was published by Freight Books in 2017. She currently lives in Montreal.

BETH MCDONOUGH trained in silversmithing at Glasgow School of Art, and completed an M.Litt in Writing Study and Practice at Dundee University. She was inaugural Writer in Residence at Dundee Contemporary Arts. She reviews and edits poetry for Dundee University Review of the Arts. Her 2016 pamphlet *Handfast* (with Ruth Aylett) was published by Mother's Milk Books.

IAN MCDONOUGH was brought up in Brora. He has published four collections, most recently *A Witch Among The Gooseberries* (Mariscat, 2014). His work has appeared in *Poetry Review, TES, Physics Review, New Writing Scotland* and *The Scotsman*. He lives with his partner and daughter in Edinburgh, where he works as a mediator and trainer.

JAMES MCGONIGAL is a Glasgow-based poet and editor. *Beyond the Last Dragon: A Life of Edwin Morgan* (2012) was Scottish Research Book of the Year. He co-edited *The Midnight Letterbox*, Carcanet's selection of Morgan's correspondence 1950–2010. *The Camphill Wren* (Red Squirrel Press, 2016) and *Turning Over in a Strange Bed* (Mariscat Press, 2017) are his most recent collections.

COLIN MCGUIRE is a poet and performer from Glasgow, who lives in Edinburgh. He has three collections: *everybody lie down and no-one gets hurt* (Red Squirrel Press, 2013), *As I sit quietly, I begin to smell burning* (2014) and *Enhanced fool disclosure* (Speculative Books, 2018). He won the 'Out:spoken' award for the 'film poetry' category and best poetry overall in London in 2018. He is a mindfulness meditation practitioner.

JANE MCKIE's collections are *Morocco Rococo* (Cinnamon Press, 2007), *When the Sun Turns Green* (Polygon, 2009), and *Kitsune* (Cinnamon Press, 2015). She won the 2011 Edwin Morgan poetry prize. Her most recent pamphlet is *From the Wonder Book of Would You Believe It?* (Mariscat Press, 2016). She is a Lecturer in Creative Writing at the University of Edinburgh.

ELSPETH MCLEAN grew up in Edinburgh and now lives in Liverpool. She won North End Writers' 2011 *Nature in the City* competition, and has produced two pamphlets: *The Aquatic Ape* (2015) with Shirley Jones, and *Backs to the Wall* (2017) as 'Elspeth Accordion'.

HUGH MCMILLAN comes from Penpont and is a well-published poet and award-winning poet. His selected poems *Not Actually Being in Dumfries* have been published by Luath and in 2017 he was Writer-in-Residence of the Harvard Summer School in Greece.

THERESA MUÑOZ was born in Vancouver and now lives in Edinburgh. Her debut collection *Settle* was shortlisted for the Melita Hume Poetry Prize. She reviews books for *The Herald* and is Research Associate at the NCLA.

DONALD S MURRAY's books include *The Guga Hunters, And On This Rock, SY Story* (Birlinn), *Weaving Songs* (Acair) as well as *The Guga Stone* (Luath Press), *Small Expectations* (Two Ravens Press) and *Herring Tales* (Bloomsbury). His new book *The Dark Stuff* was published by Bloomsbury in April 2018.

LIZ NIVEN's collections (Canongate, then Luath) and pamphlets are in Scots and English. Awards include McCash/Herald for Scots poetry and TESS/Saltire for groundbreaking work in Scots language. The Scots dossier for European

Bureau of Lesser Used Languages was republished in 2017. She is an honorary Fellow of the Association of Scottish Literature.

DONNY O'ROURKE, born in Port Glasgow, has had overlapping careers in television, journalism and academe. A graduate of the universities of Glasgow and Cambridge he has written or edited more than a score of books, CDs and works for the theatre. Professorships, scholarships and fellowships have enabled him to travel the world, invariably by puffer...

JANET PAISLEY, who sadly died as this book was in preparation, was an award-winning Scottish poet, playwright, author, script and screen writer, writing in English and Scots. Her work was published internationally, and has been translated into 15 languages. It includes five works of historical and contemporary fiction and seven collections of poetry, the latest of which was *Sang fur the Wandert* (Luath Press).

ALASDAIR PATERSON'S most recent collections are *On the Governing of Empires* (Shearsman 2010), *Brumaire and Later* (Flarestack 2011), *Elsewhere or Thereabouts* (Shearsman 2014) and *My Life as a Mad King* (Oystercatcher 2016). He lives in Exeter, where he presents the monthly Uncut Poets event and chairs the annual Exeter Poetry Festival.

STUART A PATERSON lives by lives in Galloway. In 2017 he was appointed BBC Scotland Poet in Residence. Also in 2017, *Looking South* was published by Indigo Dreams and *Beul-fo-bhonn*, a Scots-Gaelic collaboration with Marcas Mac an Tuairneir, was published by Tapsalteerie. He has recently exhibited collaborations with stained glass artist Alec Galloway and landscape artist Simon Parkin. He works at The Stove arts hub in Dumfries.

JACOB POLLEY's fourth book of poems, *Jackself*, won the 2016 T S Eliot Prize. He was born in Cumbria, taught at the University of St Andrews until 2015, and now teaches at Newcastle University and lives with his family on the North East coast.

TOM POW's long poem *Transfusion* (Shoestring Press 2007) was in praise of another boxer, Muhammad Ali, and of Nelson Mandela. Recent publications include *Concerning the Atlas of Scotland* (Polygon and NLS) and *At The Well of Love* (Mariscat). *Barefoot: The Collected Poems of Alastair Reid*, which he edited, was published in 2018 (Galileo Publishers).

CHRIS POWICI's latest collection of poems *This Weight of Light* was published by Red Squirrel in 2015. He teaches creative writing for the University of Stirling, The Open University and gives readings and workshops for schools and writing groups. A former editor of the literary magazine *Northwords Now*, he lives in Perthshire.

SHEENAGH PUGH spent most of her life in Wales but has lived in Shetland since 2009. She has published nine collections of poetry and translations, plus a *Selected Poems* and a sort of mini-*Selected*, two novels and a critical study of fan fiction. Her new collection *Afternoons Go Nowhere* comes out from Seren in May 2019.

JOHN QUINN, an ex-teacher, writer and performer, has had poetry in *Poetry Scotland, Northwords Now, Southlight* and *Lallans* and performed work at the Dundee Literary and StAnza Poetry Festivals. His play *O Halflins an Hecklers an Weavers an Weemin* was premiered in Dundee in 2017 accompanied by Michael Marra's music. His novel *The Eyes of Grace O'Malley* (Black Wolf Books) was published in 2018.

MAGGIE RABATSKI has two pamphlet collections, *Down From The Dance* and *Holding*, published by New Voices Press. Her poems also appear in *Owersettin* (Tapsalteerie Press, 2016) alongside poems by A C Clarke and Sheila Templeton. Originally from the Western Isles, she lives in Glasgow and writes in both Gaelic and English.

KEVIN REID's poetry can be found in various online and printed publications including: *The Bee's Breakfast, Under the Radar, The Interpreter's House, The Open Mouse*, and *Ink, Sweat and Tears*. His short sequence of poems, *Burdlife*, was published by Tapsalteerie in June 2017. His latest pamphlet, *Androgyny*, was published by 4Word in May 2018. *www.eyeosphere.com*

ELIZABETH RIMMER has published three poetry collections with Red Squirrel Press, *Wherever We Live Now, The Territory of Rain* and her third, *Haggards*, which includes poems about herbs, wild landscapes, and ways of knowing as a response to social upheaval and regeneration, was published in early 2018. *www.burnedthumb.co.uk*

LYDIA ROBB's writing is inspired by the Angus countryside where she lived for many years. Awarded an SAC Bursary in 1998, she's the recipient of a number of literary prizes. She writes poetry and prose in English and Scots, and her work appears in a number of anthologies. Her collection *Last Tango with Magritte*, was published by Chapman.

JAMES ROBERTSON is a poet, novelist and editor. He is a co-founder and editor of *Itchy Coo*, the Scots language imprint for young readers. His own poetry has appeared in many pamphlets, books and other outlets. His latest publication, *Michael Marra: Arrest This Moment*, was published in October 2017.

NIKKI ROBSON is from Northern Ireland and now lives in Scotland. She holds an MLitt in Writing Practice and Study from the University of Dundee. Her poems have appeared in journals and anthologies in print and online including *Acu-*

men, *Under the Radar*, *Ink, Sweat and Tears*, *Elbow Room* and *Obsessed with Pipework*.

DILYS ROSE lives and works in Edinburgh. She is a fiction writer and poet and has published 12 books, most recently the novel *Unspeakable* (Freight Books 2017), based on the life and times of Thomas Aikenhead. Of her four poetry collections, the most recent is *Bodywork* (2007).

REBECCA SHARP is from Glasgow, currently based in Fife. Work includes *Unmapped*, poems and paintings with artist Anna King; *The Air That Carries The Weight* with Stellar Quines at the Traverse Theatre; *Rules of the Moon*, performance with sound artist Philip Jeck; and *Little Forks*, a story in English and Gaelic. www.rebeccajoysharp.com

HARRY SMART lives in Montrose. He was born in Dewsbury, in the West Riding of Yorkshire and went to school in Morley and Batley, then in 1974 to the University of Aberdeen. He has lived in Scotland since. He has published three books of poetry, *Pierrot*, *Shoah*, and *Fool's Pardon*, and one novel, *Zaire*.

IAN STEPHEN is from the Isle of Lewis. His selected poems on sea themes, *maritime*, was published by Saraband in 2016. *Waypoints – seascapes and stories of Scotland's West Coast* is a celebration of vessels, sea, land and stories, with poetry playing an integral role, published by Adlard Coles Nautical (Bloomsbury, 2017).

JUDITH TAYLOR comes from Perthshire and now lives and works in Aberdeen. She is the author of two pamphlet collections – *Earthlight* (Koo Press, 2006) and *Local Colour* (Calder Wood Press, 2010). Her first full-length collection, *Not in Nightingale Country*, was published in 2017 by Red Squirrel Press.

SHEILA TEMPLETON writes in Scots and English. A triple winner of the McCash Scots Language Poetry Competition, she has also won the Robert McLellan poetry competition and been Makar for the Federation of Writers. Her latest publications are *Owersettin*, (Tapsalteerie Press 2016) and *Gaitherin*, her first full collection (Red Squirrel Press 2016).

JACQUELINE THOMPSON's poems have appeared in *New Writing Scotland*, *Gutter*, *Poetry Ireland Review*, *The Scotsman*, and anthologies from Dundee University Press and Red Squirrel Press. She has been shortlisted for the Jane Martin Prize, Grierson Verse Prize and Westport Arts Festival Prize, and won the Neil Gunn Writing Competition 2017.

VALERIE THORNTON has two poetry collections, *Catacoustics*, and *If Only Coll Were Two Floors Down* (Mariscat Press). Internationally anthologised (poems and stories) since the 1980s, she's worked with the Royal Literary Fund since

2001. In 2012, she was awarded an Honorary Fellowship of ASLS for her writing and educational work.

TIM TURNBULL was born in North Yorkshire but has lived in Highland Perthshire for 17 years. Donut Press publish his collections *Stranded in Sub-Atomica* (2005) and *Caligula on Ice* (2009). He has also produced 'entertainments' for the stage. *Silence and Other Stories* (2016) is published by Postbox Press, the literary fiction imprint of Red Squirrel Press. His latest collection, *Avanti!* (2018), is also published by Red Squirrel Press.

RYAN VAN WINKLE is a poet, editor and live artist living in Edinburgh. His second collection, *The Good Dark*, won the Saltire Society's 2015 Poetry Book of the Year award. His poems have appeared in *New Writing Scotland*, *The Prairie Schooner* and *The American Poetry Review*.

GEORGE T WATT writes almost exclusively in Scots and has been published in *Lallans, Gutter* and *New Writing Scotland*. A past runner-up in the McCash Poetry Competition and was featured in the top 20 of 2014 by The Scottish Poetry Library. He is Membership Secretary for the Scots Language Society.

RICHARD WATT is a father of one, journalist and Dundee University graduate based in Tayside. His first solo poetry pamphlet, *The Golem*, was published by Holdfire Press of Merseyside in 2013.

ROSEANNE WATT is a poet, filmmaker and musician from Shetland. She was the winner of the 2018 Edwin Morgan Poetry Award, and runner-up in the 2018 Aesthetica Creative Writing Award. Her first collection, *Moder Dy*, will be published by Polygon in May 2019.

BRIAN WHITTINGHAM is a Glasgow-based author of poetry, short fiction and drama, and editor of anthologies and magazines. He lectures in Creative Writing and Communications at City of Glasgow College, Kelvingrove Art Gallery and Strathclyde University. Collections include *Clocking In Clocking Out* (2012) and *Bunnets 'n' Bowlers* (2009) with *Walking Between Worlds* (Red Squirrel, 2018) just published.

HAMISH WHYTE's latest collection is *Things We Never Knew* (Shoestring Press, 2016). He has edited many anthologies and runs the award-winning Mariscat Press. He is an Honorary Research Fellow in Scottish Literature, Glasgow University. He lives in Edinburgh, is convener of the city's Shore Poets and plays percussion in The Whole Shebang.

COLIN WILL is an Edinburgh-born poet with a background in botany and geology. His ninth book of poems, *The Night I Danced With Maya*, was published by Red Squirrel Press in 2017. He's a former Chair of StAnza and the Scottish

Poetry Library. *www.colinwill.co.uk*

J L WILLIAMS' first collections were *Condition of Fire* (2011) and *Locust and Marlin* (2014). *Our Real Red Selves* (Vagabond Poets, 2015) was a collaboration with two other Scottish poets. She is a performer in the poetry and music band Bright Stones, and the librettist of the opera *Snow*. Her latest poetry collection is *After Economy* (Shearsman, 2017). *www.jlwilliamspoetry.co.uk*

CHRISTIE WILLIAMSON's poems have been appearing in print and online since 2003. His debut pamphlet, *Arc o Möns* won the Calum MacDonald Memorial Award in 2010. His first full length collection *Oo an Feddirs* was published by Luath Press in 2015.

ANDREW J WILSON is an Edinburgh-based writer, editor and spoken-word performer. Recent work has appeared in *Double Bill: Poems Inspired by Popular Culture*; *Professor Challenger: New Worlds, Lost Places*; *Shoreline of Infinity*; *Dystopia Utopia Short Stories*; and *Umbrellas of Edinburgh*. With Neil Williamson, he co-edited the award-nominated anthology *Nova Scotia: New Scottish Speculative Fiction*.

JIM C WILSON's writing has been widely published for 35 years. He was Writer in Residence for Stirling District, and was a Royal Literary Fund Fellow from 2001 until 2007. He has run his Poetry in Practice classes at Edinburgh University since 1994. His most recent poetry collection is *Come Close and Listen* (Greenwich Exchange). *www.jimcwilson.com*

ROSS WILSON comes from Kelty, West Fife. His first pamphlet collection, *The Heavy Bag*, was published by Calder Wood Press in 2011. His first full collection, *Line Drawings*, was published by Smokestack Books in 2018. He lives and writes in Condorrat, North Lanarkshire, and works as an Auxiliary Nurse in Glasgow.

DAWN WOOD lives in Longforgan, Perthshire, where she works as a hypnotherapist and an artist. Her poetry collections, published with Templar Poetry, include *Quarry* (2008), *Ingathering* (2013), *Declaration* (2016) and *As Mind Imagines World* (2018). *www.dawnwoodartist.co.uk*

# Acknowledgements

Since appearing on the Scotia Extremis website, some of these poems have been reproduced in magazines, pamphlets and poetry collections. We thank the editors and publishers of these publications for their support.

Ken Cockburn's poem 'Bob the Roman' appeared in his collection *Floating the Woods* (Luath).

Robert Crawford's 'To Sullom Voe' appeared as 'Shetland' in *The Scottish Ambassador* (Cape, 2018)

Imtiaz Dharker's 'Mobarik Picnic' appears in her latest collection, *Luck is the Hook*, from Bloodaxe Books.

Graham Fulton, Harry Smart, Brian Whittingham and Jim C Mackintosh's poems appeared in the anthology *Mind the Time* (Nutmeg, 2017).

Jackie Kay's 'A Day Like Today' first appeared in *The Scotsman*.

Hugh McMillan's 'Summerisle' appeared in *Dark Horse* magazine.

Liz Niven's 'Empire' appeared in the anthology *A Kind of Stupidity* (Dove Tales, 2018)

Alasdair Paterson's 'The Royal Mile' is included in the pamphlet collection *Silent Years* (Flarestack Poets).

Stuart A Paterson's 'Nae Regrets' appeared in *The Stony Thursday Book* (Limerick Arts Council).

Sheila Templeton's 'James Keir Hardie' appeared in her collection *Gaitherin* (Red Squirrel Press).

Colin Will's 'In a Good Light' appeared in his collection *The Night I Danced With Maya* (Red Squirrel Press).

The editors are indebted to Calum Colvin for his generosity in allowing us to use his work on the cover of this book.

# **Luath** Press Limited

*committed to publishing well written books worth reading*

LUATH PRESS takes its name from Robert Burns, whose little collie Luath (*Gael.*, swift or nimble) tripped up Jean Armour at a wedding and gave him the chance to speak to the woman who was to be his wife and the abiding love of his life. Burns called one of the 'Twa Dogs' Luath after Cuchullin's hunting dog in Ossian's *Fingal*. Luath Press was established in 1981 in the heart of Burns country, and is now based a few steps up the road from Burns' first lodgings on Edinburgh's Royal Mile. Luath offers you distinctive writing with a hint of unexpected pleasures.
Most bookshops in the UK, the US, Canada, Australia, New Zealand and parts of Europe, either carry our books in stock or can order them for you. To order direct from us, please send a £sterling cheque, postal order, international money order or your credit card details (number, address of cardholder and expiry date) to us at the address below. Please add post and packing as follows: UK – £1.00 per delivery address; overseas surface mail – £2.50 per delivery address; overseas airmail – £3.50 for the first book to each delivery address, plus £1.00 for each additional book by airmail to the same address. If your order is a gift, we will happily enclose your card or message at no extra charge.

**Luath** Press Limited
543/2 Castlehill
The Royal Mile
Edinburgh EH1 2ND
Scotland
Telephone: +44 (0)131 225 4326 (24 hours)
Email: sales@luath. co.uk
Website: www. luath.co.uk